SINGLE & SECURE

Break Up with the Lies and Fall in Love with the Truth

Rich Wilkerson Jr.

Published in Miami, Florida by VOUS Church

ISBN 978-0-578-98777-4
ISBN (eBook) 978-0-578-31355-9

1st Printing
Printed in the United States of America

intothenight.com

This book is dedicated to my three children,
Wyatt, Wilde, and Waylon.
May you be secure in every season.

As you read this book,
I want to help you, encourage you,
and answer your questions.
Feel free to text me 305-501-1890.

CONTENTS

YOUR BEST DAYS

Have you ever been standing in line for a ride at an amusement park when they let single riders skip to the front?

This usually happens when ride operators want to move the line along by filling up empty seats. Some hyper-efficient attendant yells out, "Any single riders here?" Then a few lonely souls awkwardly squeeze to the front while everyone else stares at these misfits who either came alone or don't care to wait until they can ride with their friends. As if that walk of shame isn't bad enough, the solo riders usually end up being third wheels, squeezed in next to families or couples who feel like their personal space is being invaded.

The single rider system is fine for amusement parks. Who cares, right? If you want to ride solo, it's not a big deal. And if people look at you funny, ignore them. After all, you're getting twice the rides they are out of that admission ticket.

Here's my point, though. In real life, the "single riders" shouldn't be seen as the weird ones, the misfits, the third wheels. If you are single, you can choose to remain single or to marry, and that choice has zero impact on your value or potential as a person.

And yet, no one seems to treat you that way. If you're like many singles I've talked to, people are constantly telling you that you need to get married. Of course they should mind their own business, but you can't tell them that, so you just smile and try to change the topic. These awkward conversations might be what you dread most about holidays and family reunions because nobody misses an opportunity to make a pointed joke at your expense. It gets old quickly.

I'd like to propose that not only is it unrealistic for someone to subtly (or not so subtly) pressure you to find a spouse, it's actually toxic. This whole "everyone should find love, get married, and start a family" mindset is unhealthy, unbiblical, and unrealistic. It implies that your best days are in the future, that today is just a holding pattern until you find the special someone who will meet you at the altar and walk with you into your happily ever after.

This toxic perspective of singleness hurts people. Over the years, DawnCheré and I have spoken on countless topics, and the talks that get the most response, the YouTube videos that get the most views, and the question-and-answer sessions that arouse the most emotion, are the ones that address this crazy stage of life called singleness. These responses speak to the confusion and pain many people feel, and they also highlight the fact that even in the church—or worse, *especially* in the church—singles feel pressured to choose a life partner as soon as possible. There is an expectation that "normal" life means school, graduation, career, marriage, and kids, more or less in that order.

That is precisely the reason you need to break away from the myths and stereotypes of singleness: because there is no such thing as normal. And if there were, why would we assume that normal is the goal, anyway? Striving to be average and unremarkable seems like an effective way to *lose* your life, not to find it.

The goal of this book, therefore, is not to convince you to get married. It's not to give you a list of steps, keys, principles, magic spells, or love potions so you can find a partner and live happily ever after. I simply want to help you be confident and content with where you are now.

That's the best way to enjoy today, and it's also the most effective launchpad for tomorrow, whether or not tomorrow includes a spouse. After all, if you can't enjoy your current life, you probably won't enjoy your future life. Contentment comes from learning to find value in the season you're experiencing today. Being single is *immensely* valuable. It's a beautiful, fun, productive stage of life that often doesn't get enough credit.

It might seem odd for a married person to talk about the joys of singleness. I don't secretly wish I were single. I love marriage. (And no, my wife didn't make me say that.) But I also get a little tired of hearing people insinuate that marriage and family are the pinnacles of life and godliness and that you are somehow incomplete until you've started a family of your own. That's a myth that needs to be debunked.

Ironically, my own story is about as far from prolonged singleness as you can get. I was seventeen when I met DawnCheré. Now that I'm a parent, I realize more than ever how crazy that sounds. But hey, when you know, you know.

Also ironic is the fact that only two months before, I had recommitted my life to God and decided to stop pursuing romance and instead pursue Jesus. God must have been laughing at that. It turns out you can do both at the same time.

Anyway, I first met DawnCheré in Nashville, where I was visiting my brother, who was performing at a church musical event. At some point during the performance, I idly looked up toward the balcony and found myself instantly enthralled with the most beautiful blonde bombshell I'd ever seen. Her hair waved softly in some invisible wind, golden light illuminated her perfect face, and she moved in dramatic slow motion while the *Titanic* theme song played in the background.

At least, that's how I remember it.

Actually, she was probably just sitting there listening to worship music, unaware that some dude down below was falling in love with her even before the closing prayer.

Her name was DawnCheré Duron, and for me, it was love at first sight. For her? Not so much. That's something she still holds over my head. I had to win her heart, which I eventually did.

Our dating years were a beautiful, romantic journey punctuated by moments of stark terror, mostly because she broke up with me multiple times—sometimes for a day, sometimes for a month. (I still hold *that* over her head. At least we both have some leverage in this relationship. That's healthy, isn't it?) After nearly five years of dating, we were married in 2006. I was twenty-two; she was twenty-one.

A few years into our marriage, we discovered that it would be difficult, maybe impossible, to have children. I'll share more about that in the next chapter, but for now, let me say that while we waited and prayed and waited some more, we learned a lot of things we didn't learn as singles, simply because we married so young. It was a different kind of waiting for us, a different type of pain and confusion, but there are a lot of parallels.

The funny thing about hard seasons is that when you're in them, they feel as if they might last forever. They seem to be a waste, like you're spinning your wheels, unable to move backward, forward, or sideways. Years later, though, you find yourself looking back on that time with gratitude. And maybe with a little trauma, to be honest—but how boring life would be without some suspense along the way, right?

This book is the result of what DawnChéré and I have learned through many of these up-and-down seasons of our own lives, along with biblical principles, plus countless conversations with singles and couples over the years. Our story is not your story, and your story is not someone else's story; but I hope you'll find encouragement and inspiration in the pages that follow, no matter what your journey has been so far or what your future holds.

Remember, your best days aren't the ones that lie ahead, somewhere on the other side of romance, a career, or a family. Your best days are the ones you're living now. That's all you've got, after all. You might not be a single rider forever—who can know?—but if you are one today, own it. Make the most of it. Celebrate it. Enjoy it.

Your best days are the days you live to the fullest. That starts now.

01
SINGLE AND STUCK

I'LL NEVER FORGET THE SIGHT: my beloved Jeep Wrangler up to its axles in mud, futilely spinning its tires, digging deeper and deeper into the flooded trail with each punch of the accelerator. No one had warned me this could happen, so I was emotionally unprepared for the moment. Worse, I was physically unprepared—I didn't have a tow rope or a winch. I also didn't have any experience driving in the mud.

I was a college student, single and carefree, going to school in Cleveland, Tennessee. Some friends had convinced me that my 4x4 Jeep with its oversized tires and jacked-up suspension was perfect for "mudding." I had no idea what mudding was, which in retrospect should have been a red flag. They explained that it meant going off-road. They did it all the time, they assured me. We would find flooded fields and muddy trails and test the limits of our endurance. It would be the triumph of man over nature.

More like the triumph of nature over stupidity, as it turned out.

Those upgrades to the tires and suspension were purely about style, by the way, because I've always been more of a city guy than a back-roads adventurer. But according to my friends, the upgrades made me and my Jeep virtually invincible. I could climb mountains. I could cross rivers. The gates of hell itself could not prevail against me. They promised me a weekend I'd never forget.

They were right, but for all the wrong reasons.

That weekend, we went off road and off the grid. There were two of us with vehicles, plus a couple of passengers, and for an hour and a half, we had an incredible time. We spun donuts, we scared crows and cows, we caught air, we gave ourselves whiplash. It was amazing. Then we came to a giant trench of mud, deeper and wider than anything we had attempted so far.

"Rich, I think you can drive across that," one of them said.

"Yeah, absolutely," another one added.

"Wait, you *think*? Or you're sure?" It was the first time I had done this, after all, so I was relying on their good judgment.

"Bro, you're good," said the third.

The vote was unanimous, so I put the Jeep in drive and hit the gas. That's when I discovered that when it comes to a bunch of nineteen-year-old adrenaline junkies, "unanimous" means absolutely nothing. We made it six feet through the mud before the Jeep came to a complete halt. In a panic, I revved the RPMs way too high and succeeded in digging my own soggy grave.

I got out to take a look. It was bad. The entire Jeep was sitting at an angle, my front right tire sunk halfway to the center of the earth, my back left tire up in the air. Mud was everywhere, and the hole I'd excavated gave new meaning to the phrase "deep South."

"Rich, don't worry," my friends said. "We'll tow you out."

"Oh, really? How are you going to do that?" I asked. At this point, I was starting to realize their confidence was based mostly on hormones and energy drinks, not on actual experience or common sense.

"I have a cable in my truck," one of my buddies said. He pulled his vehicle to the edge of the mud. Then he dug around in the back for a minute and returned with an extension cord. Not a towing cable, not a coil of wire, not a rope, but a literal extension cord.

"Bro, are you kidding? What are you going to do, plug in a coffee maker?"

"This will work, you'll see." He tied one end to my Jeep, the other to his. I sat in the driver's seat and prayed for a miracle.

It didn't work, of course. The moment he hit the gas, the cord pulled taut and then snapped like a piece of spaghetti. Score: Nature 1, City Boys 0.

You might think that my point with this story is that if you have stupid problems, it could be because you have stupid friends. That would be a valid point. But it's not the one I want to make. The moral is this:

> When you're stuck, you need something stronger than you and stronger than what you're stuck in to pull you out.

That is easy enough to understand when it comes to a 4x4 buried in a muddy Tennessee field. But it gets more complex, more nuanced, when it comes to the figurative "stuckness" we experience from time to time in our lives. Why? Because it can be hard to know if we are even stuck in the first place, and if we are, what is causing it.

STUCK OR SECURE?

Feelings can be deceptive. Sometimes we feel stuck because nothing has changed on the outside, but God is actually doing life-changing work inside of us. Other times, we can feel like we're moving a hundred miles an hour because life is so full, but we're really just spinning our wheels and going nowhere.

It gets even more complicated when you're navigating life as a single adult, with all the transitions, learning curves, and expectations singleness entails. Maybe you feel stuck right now in relationships, dating, finances, career, life goals, education, or some other area. If so, do your feelings of stuckness indicate a problem to be fixed, an invitation to grow, or just a passing mood? Do you need to quit something, start something, change something, or just stick it out? How is that frustration connected to your relationship status, or is it connected at all?

These are questions we all wrestle with, single or not. If you've felt anxiety, impatience, or frustration in any of the above areas, it means you're human and alive—both of which are positives.

At the same time, it may be that you don't feel stuck at all. In fact, you are delighted with who you are and how life is going. I hope so. However, if you do feel trapped or frustrated when it comes to being single, I'd like to share a few thoughts about how you might go from "single and stuck" to "single and secure."

Over the years, DawnCheré and I have met with thousands, of single adults. Many have expressed that they feel at a standstill in their lives. For one reason or another, they don't see a clear path forward, they feel powerless to make changes, or their life isn't what they expected. Often, they connect those feelings to the fact that they are single.

They often feel boxed in by expectations, stuck between where they are and where everyone thinks they should be.

> They often feel lost between categories. They aren't the crazy kids they used to be, but they aren't the stable adults they plan to be either. They are in limbo between the two.
>
> They often feel confused about life. They are trying to decide what they believe about self, God, love, purpose, career, morality, and so much more—and it's overwhelming.
>
> They often feel paralyzed about the future. They don't know how to make plans or move forward because they know that marriage and kids could change everything.

Here's the thing, though. It's a big jump to go from "I'm stuck and single" to "I'm stuck *because* I'm single." Just because two things exist simultaneously doesn't mean one is caused by the other. That's called a false corollary. You could also be married and stuck, rich and stuck, educated and stuck, well-traveled and stuck, famous and stuck, influential and stuck, mudding and stuck. You get the idea.

On the other hand, you could be any of the above things and also be *free.* Neither freedom nor frustration is necessarily tied to your marital status or any other state or stage of life.

Connecting "single" to "stuck" means you've placed the weight of your emotional health, or your financial stability, or your life plans (or all of the above) on a significant other, on

Here's the thing, though. It's a big jump to go from "I'm stuck and single" to "I'm stuck *because* I'm single." Just because two things exist simultaneously doesn't mean one is caused by the other.

some person you hope can pull you out of the mud.

That's too much weight to put on any relationship. Relationships aren't meant for that, and they don't work like that. It's not fair to the other person, but maybe more importantly, it's not fair to you.

You are stronger than that. You don't need someone to save you because Jesus already did that, and he continues to help you every day. Too often, people are willing to go to any lengths to find that special someone, including losing who they are in the process. That's not okay.

One of the most important truths we're going to explore in this book is that you are enough just as you are, in Christ, with or without a life partner. You are valuable, whole, and needed. No human connection could add to who you are. You don't need a relationship to fix you, heal you, free you, or satisfy you. You are complete now. Period.

> Relationships don't complete you. They complement you.
> Relationships don't define you. They develop you.
> Relationships don't control your life. They beautify your life.
> Relationships don't make you valuable. They add value to who you already are.

If you feel single and stuck in life, the problem is not your lack of a spouse. If you're married and stuck, the problem is not your spouse or kids. Don't look to external, human sources for something only Jesus can provide. And don't blame what only you can change on someone else.

If you look to a relationship to fix you or make you secure, it will snap long before it gets you out of your emotional hole. The opposite is true as well: you can't pull anyone else out of their mess, no matter how loving and patient and kind you are. You are not their savior. Jesus is.

Relationships were never meant to be a cure-all for life's problems. That is one of the great myths of love and singleness, and it's subtly propagated by everything from romcoms to reality dating shows to Disney princess movies. If two dysfunctional, combative, selfish people get married, they don't magically get along just because they have great chemistry or passionate sex. They just combine their dysfunction under one roof.

I don't mean to sound cynical. There is nothing more important than love in this life, and I think romantic love may be the most beautiful love of all. But until we find our confidence and completeness in God's love, it's going to be difficult, even impossible, to be secure in ourselves and to love others as we are meant to love them. Why? Because we'll always be trying to fulfill our need for love and acceptance by turning to humans. And humans can't handle that kind of pressure any more than an extension cord can pull a two-ton Jeep out of a muddy grave.

Relationships aren't the only extension cords we turn to when we feel stuck, of course. We might hang our hopes on finding a new job, getting more education, moving to a new city, making new friends, or starting a new hobby. While those things could be helpful, they can't save us. External changes can't fix internal issues.

- Finding the love of your life doesn't solve loneliness.
- Being hired for your dream job won't eliminate financial pressure.
- Having more sex won't give your life meaning.
- Alcohol, food, or exercise won't heal trauma from the past.
- Moving to another city won't make you more disciplined.
- Quitting your job won't take away all your stress.
- Having children won't satisfy your need for love.

None of these things, in and of themselves, can fix what is broken or lacking inside of you. They might help, but none of them can take you from stuck to secure. Why? Because they are finite, limited, temporary, human. Only God is God.

YOU'RE NOT MISSING ANYTHING

So, what is strong enough to take us from stuck to secure? I'm sure you've already figured out the answer: it's only and always Jesus. Jesus said to his disciples:

> Remain in me, as I also remain in you. No branch can bear fruit by itself; it must remain in the vine. Neither can you bear fruit unless you remain in me....As the Father has loved me, so have I loved you. Now remain in my love. (John 15:4,9)

Jesus was saying that they were complete in him. Their joy was full in him. Nothing the world had to offer could add to what they already had in Jesus, and nothing could take it away. They didn't need anything or anyone else, just Jesus.

No matter how stuck you feel, no matter how frustrated you might be, no matter how much life seems to have let you down, in God, you already have what you need to move forward.

You are not missing anything.

Think about that for a moment. Say it to yourself a couple of times until you believe it. "I am not missing anything. I am not broken. I am not a failure or an embarrassment or a weakling or any other negative label I might have let creep into my head. Don't let the pressure, the shame, or the expectations of others tell you otherwise.

Yes, you have a lot to learn. No, you are not perfect. Yes, you might feel frustrated right now. No, life doesn't always make sense. But none of these things change the baseline reality that Jesus loves you and is with you.

Jesus loves you

It will get easier.
You will be okay.
Things will start to make sense.
You will find forward momentum.
You will look back and see growth.

Of course, saying that we are complete in Jesus doesn't mean we should forget about everyone else. We are not worlds unto ourselves, solitary little planets sailing through the void of space. That sounds dark and cold and terrifying.

We need other people. God calls us to love each other, help each other, learn from each other, build into each other. We have to do that from a place of sufficiency in Jesus, though, or it won't work.

God loves us first, and his love is what makes everything else work. It is what takes us from stuck to secure. The apostle John wrote:

> This is how God showed his love among us: He sent his one and only Son into the world *that we might live through him.* This is love: not that we loved God, but that he loved us and sent his Son as an atoning sacrifice for our sins. Dear friends, since God so loved us, we also ought to love one another. No one has ever seen God; but if we love one another, God lives in us and *his love is made complete in us.* (1 John 4:9-12, emphasis added)

John states that Jesus came to earth "that we might live through him." While that phrase refers ultimately to eternal life, Jesus made it clear that he came to give us abundant life starting now, not just after death (John 10:10). In other words, as soon as Jesus became part of our day-to-day experience, we began truly living. That abundance continues to be found in him and through him. Our sufficiency and completeness are in Jesus, not in anything or anyone else.

That's not all. If we love God, we will love one another. You can't love God and not love those around you, and the very fact we love one another means God lives in us and "his love is made complete in us."

Notice the order here: God loves us first, and that enables us to love others. Love starts with God, ends with God, and points to God. His love is what makes us complete, and because of that completeness, we are free to love.

Do you want to feel secure rather than stuck? Don't start by finding someone to love you or someone to love, or by filling your life with hobbies, friends, entertainment, or career. Start by finding yourself in the love of God. Everything flows from that.

How do we learn to depend on God's love this way? How do we grow in our confidence in him? Often, it happens in the waiting seasons, in moments when life doesn't make a lot of sense, when hopes go unrealized, when faith feels empty, when confusion and even anger rise up within us because what we expected to happen didn't. In those moments, God becomes more real than ever because we turn to him for who he is, not just for what he gives us. We find completeness in him even when, or especially when, our experiences contradict our expectations.

For DawnChеré and I, never has this truth of finding completeness in God been more clearly illustrated than in our journey of infertility. We've shared the story publicly on a couple of occasions, but for the most part, it's been a private and very personal experience. I realize this might not feel directly applicable to your stage in life, and I'm not trying to compare our pain to anyone else's pain. I'd like to share some of our story here, though, in the hope that what we learned about depending on God's love and waiting through difficult seasons might encourage you in your own experiences of frustration or hurt.

OUR STORY OF INFERTILITY

We had been married for about three years when we decided to start trying to have children. When months went by and DawnCheré didn't become pregnant, we weren't too worried about it. We were young, life is long, and the thought never crossed our minds that conceiving children could be a problem. Eventually, DawnCheré had some blood tests done just to be sure there weren't any underlying issues.

The day she received the results was August 11th, her twenty-fifth birthday. She had to work that day, so she scheduled the appointment early, around eight o'clock. When the doctor came into the room, the look on her face was serious, subdued. The test results had come back irregular, she explained, which didn't make sense because DawnCheré didn't fit the profile of what the tests seemed to indicate.

The doctor wanted my wife to see an infertility specialist right away. She did, and the specialist broke the news to us: it would be difficult, if not impossible, for us to have children.

It didn't even sink in at first. It was like we were hearing news about someone else. It's hard to put into words the range of emotions we experienced in the days that followed. Then the days became months, and the months became years, and the implications of our diagnosis were all too real. We prayed a lot and cried more than once. We went to doctor after doctor, tried medicine after medicine, and procedure after procedure. On several occasions, we were sure we were pregnant only to receive the phone call we came to dread: *not pregnant.*

While the situation was complicated and confusing, I can't say we lived under a cloud of pain or loss. Yes, there were times of questions and sorrow, and there were heavy moments of disappointment when pregnancy test results were negative; but over-

We realized that our pain was private, but our condition was public. That is, people could see what was going on, but they couldn't understand what we were feeling.

all, we experienced peace and joy beyond our understanding. It was the grace of God. The circumstances were challenging, but the pain never defined us, and the loss never stole our security. As the years passed, we continually found strength, safety, and peace in God.

We had to. There was nowhere else to turn.

It's funny because when you're single, everyone asks when you're going to start dating. When you're dating, they ask when you're going to get married. When you get married, they ask when you're going to have a baby. When you have one baby, they ask when you're going to have the second. It never ends. Most people don't mean anything by it, but those questions can be painful when you're wondering the same thing but feel powerless to change your situation.

We realized that our pain was private, but our condition was public. That is, people could see what was going on, but they couldn't understand what we were feeling. We didn't even tell people for the longest time because we didn't want to be objects of pity. I'd make jokes when people would ask about kids: "Hey, we're practicing every day! But it's in God's hands." Everyone would laugh, me included. Inside, though, the struggle was real.

As I look back, there were a few decisions we made along the way that helped us immensely. I share them not to compare pain or to pretend I have all the answers, but because these principles transcend one situation or one story.

First, we decided to *find our happiness and our identity in God, not a baby.* We ignored the whispers of shame that told us we were somehow second-class humans because we didn't fit the mold of a typical family. That's harder than it sounds, by the way. We could not base our self-worth on parenthood. Even if we never had children, we were enough. God was enough. The blessing wasn't the baby—the blessing was Jesus.

We also decided to *be the best version of ourselves*, no

matter what happened. We were going to live to the fullest; we were going to fulfill our potential; we would be complete and confident and joyful whether or not we ever had children. We refused to let our peace depend on something outside of our control. We rejected fear when it crept into our thoughts. This wasn't easy, and it took us a few years to come to a place of complete confidence. It brought so much rest, though, to simply focus on what we could control and to make the most of what we had, rather than second-guessing God or ourselves all the time.

We decided to *celebrate the blessings that people around us received.* Family get-togethers were tough, especially when siblings who were married after us began having children before us. The same thing happened at church as people around us had children, and year after year, we were still barren. Instead of allowing jealousy or resentment to control us, though, we decided to rejoice with them, to be genuinely happy for them, to hug their babies even tighter, and to honor what God had done for them. Why should we miss out on the joy around us just because we hadn't yet seen the answer to our own prayers? Knowing how to celebrate others' successes and miracles not only unlocks our ability to enjoy the present more, it prepares us to receive our own miracle in the future.

Finally, we decided to *let God write our story, not somebody else's story.* DawnCheré loves surprises, and she decided early on in the journey that she'd rather wait for God's surprises in our lives than wish we had the story someone else was living. There is so much freedom in that! We didn't have to compare ourselves. We could simply live this life, *our* life, the gift God had given us, and trust that he had good things in store.

Eight years after our diagnosis, we received another phone call. This one was different. *You're pregnant.* Like the initial news years before, it took a while to sink in. But we had nine months for that to happen, and with each day, each stage, each kick inside DawnCheré's belly, the pain faded into memory and the miracle became our reality.

Wyatt Wesley Wilkerson was born on January 23, 2018. A year and a half later, God gave us double for our trouble when Wilde Wesley Wilkerson joined our family on October 25, 2019. And on July 2, 2021, we welcomed our baby girl Waylon Wesley Wilkerson. Now our lives are full of joy and severely lacking in sleep, but we wouldn't have it any other way. God has been good to us.

GOD IS ENOUGH

Maybe you've been waiting years for a spouse, or a career, or a healing, or some other dream. I understand the pain and frustration. I know what it means to watch the years go by and feel left behind by life. I can't promise that your story will have the ending you desire, but I can promise that God is with you and that his plans for you are perfect. Find your completeness in him, even when life seems like one big contradiction.

There is something beautiful about how God reveals himself to us not only through his blessings but also through our waiting. He's not a genie in a bottle, after all, obligated to grant us the wishes and whims of our hearts. He is our God. He is our good Father. Yes, he knows what we want, but he also knows what we need, what we are capable of, what we are called to, and what we can accomplish.

What we need most are not the blessings our hearts wish for so deeply at times, but the God of all blessings himself. God is the only true source of satisfaction, the reason we can be secure and complete. The blessings God gives are just icing on the cake.

You might be single, but you're not stuck. Being single is your blessing, not your problem. It is not an obstacle to your happiness.

It's so tempting during those times when life doesn't make sense to wonder if God cares or if he is even real. He does care and he is real. Lean into the grace God gives for each day. Don't overthink the future—it's overwhelming. But today, right now, God's faithfulness is your portion. He is enough.

Jesus is more than enough for any need, any stage, any frustration, any failure. That's not a lesson just for singleness: it's a lesson for life. You are loved by Jesus and you are complete in Jesus. So if you feel single and stuck, or stuck being single, or stuck because you're single, or sick of being stuck and single, or any other combination of those words, you probably need to adjust your mindset.

You might be single, but you're not stuck. Being single is your blessing, not your problem. It is not an obstacle to your happiness. It is not an awkward stage between childhood and adulthood. It's not something to be despised, survived, rushed through, or resented.

Being single is beautiful. It is valid and fulfilling and powerful, and it deserves to be celebrated, which we'll talk about in the next chapter.

Forget single and stuck.

You're single and secure.

JHEANELLE'S STORY

What is security and success by the world's standards? Good paying job, active social life, great looking partner, and so on? It's crazy to think that my earliest memories of success, security, or completeness always included a partner. Whoever heard of a woman being all those things on her own? Crazy, right? From middle school Valentine's Day candygrams to Hallmark cards, romcoms, and those teen romance sections in your favorite bookstore, the idea of needing two to make something complete has been abundantly clear to us. Needless to say, this can quickly cause some disorientation. Single and secure, however, are not mutually exclusive terms. You can be one and the other at the same time.

Looking back, I have always been a romantic. I had it all planned out. Meet, date, and marry my high school sweetheart. Have successful careers, an active social life, three kids, and a white picket fence. Oh, and I can't forget the dog—gotta have a dog (which is crazy, because I'm afraid of dogs). As I've grown and been exposed to a variety of different viewpoints, I've come to the startling conclusion that the world lies to us. It lies so much and so loud that you begin to believe the lies. As a woman, especially, it paints this picture of insecurity: if you're single, there must be a problem with you.

I'll turn thirty in a few months. I know that for a lot of women, that brings a sense of pressure, but I've learned something that has helped to reduce some of that pressure. Being single is not a problem. It's not an issue. And being single and secure is not a myth or a lie you have to tell yourself. It's who you can actually be.

I thank God that I found my way back to him because living in this world and thinking like this world broke me. It caused me to be insecure. I felt weak, ashamed, unloved, and unwanted. I felt ugly. With God, everything is the opposite. I am loved, I am wanted, I am strong. I am who he says I am, and if I'm made in his image, how can I be anything other than beautiful? I mean, have you seen his creation?

In him, I am secure. I also happen to be single, but that isn't a period, a pause, or a stop. Things are not at a halt. Paul had it right: we all have our gifts, and right now, being a single woman is a gift. I have the opportunity to fully focus on specific things in this season of my life. I'm not slowing down and I'm not missing out. I know he'll come one day, and when he does, I hope he has to chase me because I'll be busy running after the things that God has for me.

02
IT'S YOUR PARTY

I'M SURE YOU'VE HEARD this lyric from a song popularized by Lesley Gore in the 1960s: "It's my party, and I'll cry if I want to."[1]

Sing that line to yourself a few times if you haven't heard it in a while. Catchy, isn't it? It gets stuck in your head and never leaves. You may need to listen to the rest of the song now just to get some closure.

Despite being written years before many of us were born, the words—and the emotion and heartbreak behind them—still resonate. The song connects with our need to *own* the current situation, imperfect as it might be, and to *respond* authentically. To admit and validate our feelings, even when they don't match the expectations of those around us.

Sometimes that means crying when people expect us to be happy, but it can also mean being happy when others expect us to cry, being at peace when people tell us we should be worried, or being content in life when others think we should change something.

In other words, it's your life, and you get to choose how to live it and how to feel about it—which means the choice to make the most of singleness is up to *you.* No one else can live your life for you.

> You own your singleness.
> You own your decisions.
> You own your body.
> You own your emotions.
> You own your time.
> You own your relationships.

God's will comes first, of course, so I'm not talking about living selfishly or independently from him. When I talk to singles about the issues they are facing, though, it often seems that their problem isn't caring too little about what God thinks, but caring too much about what other people think.

Maybe it's happened to you. In a well-meaning attempt to

be wise and humble, you end up adopting negative views of yourself. Of your ideas. Of your maturity. Of what God wants to do in and through you. You let cultural, social, or family expectations—that don't necessarily reflect God's expectations—skew your self-view and life choices.

You need to give yourself more credit, and you need to trust the work God is doing in you.

> Your life is your party, and you can cry if you want to.
> You can also laugh if you want to.
> Or take a vacation.
> Or read a book.
> Or write a book.
> Or speak out when you see injustice.
> Or ask hard questions about your beliefs.
> Or change majors halfway through college.
> Or raise awareness about a social need.
> Or adopt a pet.
> Or buy a phone that wasn't made by Apple.
> Or go on a blind date.
> Or get a new job.
> Or stay at this job because quitting is overrated.
> Or move out of your parents' house.
> Or stay with your parents but put a lock on the bedroom door because moving out is also overrated.

It's your life. You only get one. So make the most of it.

Starting now.

I'm not advocating that you turn your back on everyone or that you refuse to heed good advice. It's important to value the influence and wisdom of the people around you. None of us should live just for ourselves, and we'd be dumb to try. We need people. But we also need to take responsibility for our lives, and we need to develop confidence that we can and do make good choices.

You are an adult in your own right.
God speaks to you and through you.
The world needs what you have to offer.
There is a divine calling on your life.
There is divine gifting in you.
You have wisdom, perspective, and understanding.

You are enough. The world needs you to believe that about yourself. It needs you to lean into who God has called you to be and who you have grown to be, despite (or because of) the mistakes you've made along the way. God is with you, and you have so much to offer.

Not only is it your life to live, but the party is also already in full swing. Life is happening now. You don't have to wait until something changes, you reach some milestone, or you achieve some goal. If that's your attitude, you'll be waiting for a long time because you'll never feel completely ready. Honestly, I don't think any of us ever feel fully prepared for life or mature enough for the tasks ahead.

I've accepted the fact that I'll always feel at least a little bit unqualified and unprepared for the things I'm responsible for and for the choices I must make today. It's okay to occasionally feel like I'm not enough, as long as I don't let that feeling intimidate me or paralyze me.

How about you? Do you feel confused, insecure, or frustrated about where you are in life? Or are you excited, full of faith, and overflowing with dreams? Or—and this is most likely the case— a mix of both confused and excited?

[redacted] Own it

Whether your party is what you thought it would be by now or it's something completely different, it's still your party.

Would you have it any other way?

I've accepted the fact that I'll always feel at least a little bit unqualified and unprepared for the things I'm responsible for and for the choices I must make today.

SHAME GAME

One of the trickiest obstacles to owning and celebrating life as a single is the subtle layers of shame that can permeate this season. Impossible expectations, constant pressures, newbie mistakes, bad decisions, recurring anxiety—they can all combine to make singleness a breeding ground for shame, which is one of the most harmful, damaging, paralyzing feelings humans can experience.

Author and researcher Brené Brown defines shame as the "universal fear of being unworthy of love and belonging." She adds that since we have an innate need to be loved and to belong, shame could be called "the master emotion."[2] Shame is a controller. A silencer. It strikes at the heart of our identity and value.

Dr. Brown states that one of the keys to living free from shame is to develop what she calls "shame resilience," which means recognizing shame for what it is, moving through it, and growing as a result of it. While shame thrives in secrecy, she says, shame resilience comes from vulnerability, honesty, and openness.[3]

In other words, you fight shame with honesty. Cry at your party. Admit your struggles. Embrace your humanity. It's okay to be where you are now, even if you are not where you expected to be or where you plan to stay. Your struggles are not a reflection of your value as a person, and they do not imply that you are unworthy of love or belonging. Don't let shame lie to you. Don't let shame control you.

Singleness is often a hotbed for shame because built right into its definition is the implication of lack and insufficiency. Think about it. A single person is, simply and literally, an unmarried adult. Can you see the problem with that definition? As a single, you are defined by what you are not. We'll come back to that again because I think it's a real problem.

In everyday use, the definition of the term "single" is a bit fuzzier. It often refers to an adult who is not in a committed, exclusive romantic relationship. In other words, you aren't married, engaged, or seriously dating anyone. You're single and ready to mingle. Or maybe you're not ready to mingle because the whole dating scene makes you cringe, but at least you *could* if you wanted to. Theoretically. Just not right now.

Whether you define single as unmarried or unavailable, what makes being single especially difficult is how readily people around you make assumptions about what you are lacking, what you are doing wrong, or what you really want. They think they know more about you than you do, and they have no problem sharing their opinions with you.

Their not-helpful comments only add stress and guilt to an already difficult time. Maybe you've had some of the following experiences of shame:

- Unsolicited and unwelcomed advice from people who know nothing about your life but feel entitled to tell you how to fix it.
- Family members who are constantly trying to set you up with someone, as if they are doing you a favor.
- The coworker who always hits on you because you are "available," and thinks that means he or she has a chance.
- The unfunny jokes about how time is passing.
- Awkward third-wheel moments when you are hanging out with a couple but feel acutely alone.
- Conversations with married couples and parents in which you are ignored or talked down to because "you can't relate."
- Cliché solutions for finding a soul mate—trumpeted by blogs, books, songs, and even sermons—that just don't work in real life, or at least in your life.
- The subtle or not-so-subtle comments about biological

clocks and how you're not getting any younger.
- The rude evaluations of what is wrong with you by tactless people who imply it is your fault you're not married.

The last thing I want to be is another voice of shame. So if this book was a passive-aggressive gift to you from someone who falls anywhere on the list above, please know that I disagree with them. I'm not going to tell you what you're doing wrong or how to fix yourself. This book is not a handbook for dating, a survival manual for the desert of singleness, or ten steps to finally getting married so you can put singleness behind you forever.

This is an affirmation of you. Now. Not the future you—the married you, the parent you, the mature you, the successful you—but the *current* you. It's a recognition of who you are and where you are today.

I don't know what's best for you. No one else does, either. But God does, and he cares deeply about every detail of your existence. Other people may try to help, but ultimately, the source of your hope and confidence must be God.

No one else can fix you,
because you're not broken.

no one else

No one else can give you what you're missing,
because you're complete.

No one else can save you,
because Jesus did that already.

No one else can tell you what to do,
because God is the one leading you.

No one else can define you,
because you were made in God's image, not theirs.

That doesn't mean you can't receive from other people, as I

mentioned earlier. There is a lot to be said for getting counsel and growing in wisdom. Just read Proverbs and you'll realize how important it is to be humble and open to advice. I'm not talking about being arrogant; I'm talking about being confident. I'm talking about taking responsibility for your life rather than letting others define who you are or shame you for what they think you're doing wrong.

Other people are not the only voices that create shame, though. You also have to deal with the voice inside your head. Sometimes the greatest sources of doubt and stress are caused by an internal whisper that you aren't enough, that you are falling short, that you will fail. Maybe you are your own worst critic.

You can't shame yourself into your future, my friend. You can't stress yourself into a happy life. It will never work. Don't play the shame game because you'll always lose. You can't out-argue condemnation or out-reason guilt or out-debate insecurity. If you allow your expectations or those of people around you to determine your self-esteem, then you're defeated before you even start.

You can't win the shame game, but you don't have to play it in the first place. Opt out. Walk away. Turn to God, and learn to value yourself as he does. His opinion matters most. God defines you, and that definition starts and ends with love. You need to belong and you need to be loved—and that's what God does best.

In God, you have all you need to be secure and at peace with yourself. Even when you're crying at your own party. Even when you don't understand what is happening. Even when you feel like a failure.

Remember, shame finds strength in secrecy and silence, so talk to God. Be honest with him about whatever is causing you shame. God will not gaslight you, tone police you, ghost you, or cancel you. He won't censor you or ignore you. He won't mock you or punish you.

He'll listen to you. He'll validate you. He'll embrace you.

You can’t win the shame game, but you don’t have to play it in the first place. Opt out. Walk away. Turn to God, and learn to value yourself as he does.

He'll cry with you, just as Jesus wept with Mary and Martha when they lost their brother Lazarus. He'll encourage you. He'll change you. And he'll send you back out into a world that needs you, imperfect and insufficient as you might feel, because his grace is more than enough for your weaknesses.

THE MYTH OF THE MONOLITH

Eliminating shame and loving who you are means accepting—and celebrating—that you are unlike anyone else. That's why stereotypes can be incredibly harmful—because they lump you into a category called "single" and, based on that label, try to predict your needs, weaknesses, desires, and goals. They reduce you to a category that undermines your humanity and erases your individuality.

Have you ever felt like people were forcing you into one of these negative stereotypes about singles?

- Careless
- Selfish
- Desperate
- Lonely
- Irresponsible
- Poor
- Indebted
- Spoiled
- Awkward
- Rejected
- Clueless
- Damaged
- Picky
- Materialistic

- Shallow
- Distracted
- Uncommitted
- Narcissistic

If you've felt the pain of these or any other negative assumptions about singles, you understand how inaccurate and damaging they can be. No one wants to be reduced to the lowest common denominator of their sociological group. No one deserves to be despised or dismissed based on their age or season of life.

The word "monolith" in sociology refers to the tendency to lump entire groups of people together as if they were one block, all represented by the same adjectives or labels. Treating people groups as monoliths means we stereotype them, ignore their individuality, and gloss over the wide range of needs, strengths, and situations represented.

It's not a good thing. But it happens ~~far too often.~~ far too often

Singles are not a monolith. That is, just because you are single does not mean you are the same as other singles. You share the same marital status, but that's it. You're still as unique as any other human. Just think about the vast array of scenarios the "single" label has to encompass:

- You're in college, focused on your studies and social life, and you're not even thinking about a serious relationship right now.
- You didn't go to college, you started your own business, and your next goals are buying a house and building your future.
- You're taking a gap year before or after college, traveling the world, and loving life, with no desire to settle down anytime soon.
- You graduated college with stellar grades and yet can't seem to find work in your field. You're currently working a less-than-ideal job and living with your parents, and the most urgent thing on your mind is

jumpstarting your career.

- You're halfway through your MBA with your eye on a PhD, and the last thing you have time for is a relationship.
- You were in a beautiful relationship that ended unexpectedly, and you're hurt and confused, wondering what is wrong with you or if you'll find love again.
- You were in a toxic relationship and finally chose to break free, and you aren't sure you even want to go down that road again.
- You are a single parent and find it hard, perhaps even undesirable, to meet someone who could fit into your family.
- You've been single for more years than you care to remember, all your friends are married with kids, and you feel left behind (or get treated like you've been left behind).
- You are divorced or widowed and trying to navigate the dating scene again, and you aren't interested in playing the games everyone seems to play.
- You are perfectly content being single and have no intention or desire to be married, and you wish people would stop asking about it.

Can you see how impossibly broad the experience of singleness is? Any attempt to lump that many people together is necessarily flawed.

Stereotypes and labels usually do more harm than good, and yet they are so common. Friends, family, social media, and pop culture combine to tell you who you are, how you should act, what you need, and even what you're worth. But none of it is true. You are more than your age or your stage, more than a label or a stereotype.

How God sees you is what matters most, and in his eyes, you are far more than your marital status. He sees a person of infinite worth and importance. Someone with unique gifts, strengths, and calling. A son or daughter who is invaluable to him—right now and always and forever—regardless of whether or not you have a partner by your side. The psalmist marvels at being known by God this way, using words that are equally true about each one of us:

> You saw me before I was born.
> Every day of my life was recorded in your book.
> Every moment was laid out
> before a single day had passed.
> How precious are your thoughts about me, O God.
> They cannot be numbered!
> I can't even count them;
> they outnumber the grains of sand!
> And when I wake up,
> you are still with me!
> (Psalm 139:16-18 NLT)

Do you hear the passion and human dignity in those lines? That psalm was written thousands of years ago by King David, but he was tapping into the same need humans have had throughout the ages: to be valued for who we are as individuals, unique and intrinsically important, created and known and loved by God.

Single is not a monolith. It's not a label, stereotype, lid, or limit. Sure, it's a term we use—mostly for lack of a better one—but it should never box you into a particular way of thinking or acting. You are you, and you are infinitely valuable. That won't change whether you are single or married or a parent or divorced or widowed.

THREE MYTHS OF SINGLENESS

God does not share the negative view many people seem to have of singleness. Jesus himself was a single adult. Think about that for a moment. He lived for thirty-three years on this planet without a spouse or kids, and he seemed pretty happy to me. Sure, he was going to save the world, and the church was going to be his bride. But can you imagine Jesus trying to explain that concept at a Passover family reunion when everyone was pressuring him to find a girl and settle down?

We have to assume that he watched one childhood friend after another get married. Even some of his disciples, such as Peter, were married. Jesus must have felt the social pressure to start a family. He must have been lonely at times.

If anyone knows how to walk securely as a single, it's Jesus. And if anyone knows how to lead you in your season of singleness, it's Jesus. The fact that he was single and secure debunks many of the myths and stereotypes about being single. Let's take a look at three of those myths.

Singleness Is Not a Problem to Be Solved

You never see Jesus stressed out about not being married. You don't hear him complaining about how hard the dating scene is, or teaching the disciples how to be his wingmen, or having an existential crisis because he is a thirty-year-old virgin. Being single was a non-issue for him. He valued marriage, of course, but he appreciated singleness just as much.

There is an unspoken but very toxic assumption floating around that singleness is a problem to be solved, and the solution must be marriage and family. Here's the thing, though: not only is singleness *not* a problem, but marriage doesn't solve problems anyway. It just puts a ring on them.

Singleness is not an aberration, an abnormality, or an illness to cure or problem to fix. That should be a no-brainer, but many people still view singleness as inherently second-class. Even if you don't feel this way (which you likely don't), and even if you're surrounded by other happily unattached single friends, you might get the sense from family and married friends that until you're married, there is something wrong with you. You're eccentric. Weird. Off.
I think that's due in part to the very definition of being single, as I

Here's the thing, though. Not only is singleness not a problem, but marriage doesn't solve problems anyway. It just puts a ~~ring~~ Ring on them.

mentioned earlier. The term single is a catch-all word for anyone who falls outside the realm of married adults. That means it says more about what you *aren't* than what you *are*.

Not married
Not attached
Not committed
Not accompanied
Not loved
Not desired
Not wanted
Not seen
Not enough

As you can see, that train of thought gets very dark, very quickly. Obviously, you can still be enough, seen, wanted, desired, and loved even if you don't have a spouse or significant other. But let's be honest: those things are often unspoken connotations of the label, aren't they? There must be something wrong with you, or you would be married already.

That approach—defining you by what you are supposedly missing—is nothing less than toxic. I can't think of another label that does this to an entire category of people. We don't call children "unadults." We don't refer to married people as "unsingles." We don't speak of older people as "unyoung." But anyone from age eighteen onward who isn't married is called "unmarried" or "single" or "bachelor" or worse, and no one thinks twice about it. Only single people are referred to by titles that reinforce what they are perceived to be lacking. Well, I guess we call zombies "undead," but I doubt they care too much.

Bottom line: If you prefer to be single, or if the timing isn't right, or if you haven't found the right person yet (no matter how long it's been), don't let anyone treat you like you're flawed. And don't treat yourself that way. Your singleness is not a problem to be solved.

Singleness Is Not Inferior to Marriage

Not only did Jesus appear completely unfazed by his singleness, he also never suggested that married people are somehow better off than those who are single.

Many Christians seem to believe that God wants everyone to get married and start a family, and if you don't, you're somehow letting down God or the universe or the human race. The reality, though, is that marriage is not "more natural" or "more God's plan for you" than singleness. Whether married or single, you are pleasing to God and accepted by him.

Some people use God's statement to Adam that it wasn't good for him to be alone to make singleness sound like it's second-rate or even outright wrong. You are probably familiar with the story in Genesis 2. After God created Adam, he said, "It is not good for the man to be alone. I will make a helper suitable for him" (Genesis 2:18). Then he created Eve. Fortunately, the two seemed to hit it off, because it's not like there were any other options. They became the first couple, shared the first kiss, had the first sex, survived the first married quarrels, and started the first family.

Remember, though, Adam wasn't just unmarried when Eve appeared on the dating scene—he was the only human on the planet. That's an entirely different level of alone. So, unless you're reading this book after an apocalypse has wiped out the rest of humanity, your circumstances are not the same as Adam's. Yes, the principle of companionship is important, and marriage is arguably the most beautiful and intimate type of companionship. But it's not the only one. There are many human relationships available to you that don't involve vows and rings. Don't isolate yourself, but don't assume you have to get married, either.

Don't isolate yourself

Singleness Is Not a Limitation

It would be a massive understatement to say Jesus was a successful single person. He literally saved the world. That means you don't need to wait for a spouse and a house and a 401(k) before you begin fulfilling your calling or using your gifts. Start now.

I've spoken with single people who seem to view their single years as parenthetical to their history, as a side note or footnote, rather than an integral part of their story. They act as if they are in limbo, in a holding pattern, on pause, just waiting for marriage so their future can begin. But God never puts our lives on hold, and he doesn't consider any stage of our lives insignificant. He is always at work, even when we can't see what is happening. Even if you feel stuck now, I'm sure that later in life, when you have the perspective of time and experience, you'll look back in awe at how much God is doing in and through you right now.

Jesus wasn't the only successful single in the Bible. Paul was probably the most influential figure in early Christianity outside of Jesus, and he was also the most eligible bachelor. He planted countless churches and wrote a significant portion of the New Testament. Being single didn't stop him. If anything, it empowered him.

He wrote to the Corinthian church that marriage isn't something to idolize, stress over, or even worry about:

> I wish that all of you were as I am. But each of you has your own gift from God; one has this gift, another has that. Now to the unmarried and the widows I say: It is good for them to stay unmarried, as I do. But if they cannot control themselves, they should marry, for it is better to marry than to burn with passion. (1 Corinthians 7:7-9)

Note the language here. Paul makes it sound as if *getting married* is the second-best choice. It's almost as if he sees marriage as a concession or as settling for less than the ideal. He explains why later in the chapter: because single people are free to serve God without distractions (1 Corinthians 7:32-35).

Paul quickly adds that marriage isn't wrong, and it has its benefits, so he isn't saying that marriage is second-rate. Instead, he is reminding us that marriage doesn't complete us, it isn't necessary to follow God, and it has its challenges. All great points, and all things that we still need to hear two thousand years later.

Note this phrase: "each of you has your own gift from God." Paul calls *singleness* a gift, and he calls *marriage* a gift. They are different gifts, but gifts just the same. What a beautiful way to look at it.

Later, he adds this: "Nevertheless, each person should live as a believer in whatever situation the Lord has assigned to them, just as God has called them" (1 Corinthians 7:17). What is Paul saying? That your current state is valid and valuable, and you don't need to obsess about changing it.

In other words, you can get married or you can stay single—whichever you choose, however life leads you, whatever God gives you. Both options are valid. Both are gifts and callings. Both please God, both can be used by God, and both are blessed by God. That seems like a healthy perspective.

Rather than looking at singleness as a parenthesis and your current existence as somehow less valid, realize that God is writing your story right now. This chapter of your life will be unlike any other, but it is no less important to the narrative.

You won't unlock your potential today if you're waiting for tomorrow. You also won't enjoy today, or value today, or make the most of today. And that would be a shame because today is all you have.

***

This is your party, my friend. It's your life. It's a gift from God, and he's proud of you. Don't let anyone tell you otherwise, and don't let anyone tell you how you have to live or feel or think or act. That's your job to decide, and God will lead you. You are more than enough for this season.

God WILL lead YOU.

KAT ROWSE'S STORY

Adulting is hard. Period. Now add in the pressure of being single when everybody else thinks you shouldn't be, and adulting goes from being hard to being annoying, exhausting, and emotional.

My story is probably similar to many other single adults in their twenties. I dated guys in college, thinking I would probably marry one of them. I experienced heartbreak, and I became bitter towards dating for a time. If you had asked me two years ago how I was feeling about my singleness, I would have probably lied and said, "So good—I mean, who needs a man anyway, right?" But deep inside, I would never admit that I was carrying shame. I didn't think I was worthy of a "good man" because of dating mistakes I had made in the past.

It wasn't until God called me to take a giant leap of faith that I started to view my singleness in a new light. In 2018, I met a seven-year-old boy through our church's children's program who was in the foster care system. He was living in what could be considered a modern-day orphanage. As I got to know this boy, my heart broke more every day, and it wasn't long before God spoke to me with a clear conviction: I needed to open my home to him.

There I was, twenty-five years old, a single adult, about to care for a child. My immediate reaction was fear, but I quickly chose to surrender. My prayer became: "God, I don't know how the heck this is even going to be possible, but if this is really from you, then make a way. Please make it super clear, and I promise I'll obey."

That prayer changed the course of my life. My boy came to live with me Christmas 2018 and immediately started calling me "Mom." My heart was forever changed as I learned to love someone deeper than I've ever loved anyone. I wanted what was best for him, and I immediately began evaluating the guys in my life.

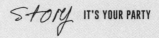

Who were the positive role models for my son? Who did I want him to be around and to learn from? Who could be a potential dad for him?

In the two years that my foster son lived with me, I did not seriously date anyone. I also didn't feel like I was missing out on anything. I learned to depend on the right community, to choose wisely who I allowed to speak into my life and my son's life, to seek God first every single day, and to rely solely on his strength when I had nothing left to give. I was walking in obedience to him and grateful that he had chosen me for such a difficult yet rewarding journey.

Looking back, I now know that God was refining me and transforming my heart to care about the things he cares about and to live the life he's destined for me to live. If I had married one of those guys I dated in college, I never would have moved to Miami, found the most incredible church community, or met my foster son. In my season of singleness, God has done more work in and through my life than I ever thought possible. He's healed me, chosen me, and invited me to be a part of his plan in this world, and I could not be more content and grateful. I now live daily with this conviction: I only get one life, and I'm not about to waste it.

03 A TALE OF THREE SINGLES

OPRAH WINFREY IS MORE than just a media personality, she is a legend, a force, a groundbreaking and ceiling-breaking woman who has taught millions of people how to lead better, more fulfilling lives. She's also a personal hero of mine, and I cannot say enough about my admiration and respect for her.

The funny thing is, her given name is not Oprah. She has one of the most recognized names in the world, but we've all been pronouncing it wrong.

Her real name is Orpah.

Orpah Winfrey. It just doesn't have the same ring, does it?

She was named after an obscure biblical character from the book of Ruth in the Old Testament. But ever since she was a child, people unfamiliar with the name accidentally called her Oprah, and it stuck. To quote her: "On the birth certificate it is Orpah, but then it got translated to Oprah, so here we are."[4]

If you read Ruth and Orpah's story in the Bible, you'll realize why Orpah was forgettable. Maybe you're familiar with it, but if not, here's a quick summary. It's a fascinating tale of three women whose lives were linked by marriages, tragedies, and faith.

Thousands of years ago, there was a famine in the land of Israel. A married couple named Elimelech and Naomi moved with their two sons to the country of Moab. Elimelech ended up dying there, but the family stayed and the two sons eventually married local women named Orpah and Ruth.

In time, both sons also died. Now all three women were widows. In that culture and time, marriage and children meant everything for a woman. The family was a source of social status, financial stability, pride, value, and importance. So, by the norms of society, these three single women had nothing.

Ruth didn't settle for that, though. That's what I want you to see in this story. There was something different about her. As you study her life, everything about her shouts that she was a secure woman of God. In a culture where being single brought

single and secure

shame, she was single and secure.

When Naomi heard that Israel was no longer suffering from famine, she decided to return. Here is how the Bible describes what happened next.

> With her two daughters-in-law she left the place where she had been living and set out on the road that would take them back to the land of Judah.
>
> Then Naomi said to her two daughters-in-law, "Go back, each of you, to your mother's home. May the Lord show you kindness, as you have shown kindness to your dead husbands and to me. May the Lord grant that each of you will find rest in the home of another husband."
>
> Then she kissed them goodbye and they wept aloud and said to her, "We will go back with you to your people."
>
> But Naomi said, "Return home, my daughters. Why would you come with me? Am I going to have any more sons, who could become your husbands? Return home, my daughters; I am too old to have another husband. Even if I thought there was still hope for me—even if I had a husband tonight and then gave birth to sons— would you wait until they grew up? Would you remain unmarried for them? No, my daughters. It is more bitter for me than for you, because the Lord's hand has turned against me!" (Ruth 1:7-13)

These three single women were at a crossroads, both literally and figuratively. They were facing a life that looked nothing like what they expected, wondering what to do next.

You can't blame Naomi for being cynical. She had suffered a lot. First famine, then uprooting her life and home, then her husband's death, and finally the death of her two sons. I'm sure Ruth and Orpah were hurt by life too. The past was painful, the present was lonely, the future was hopeless—their lives were anything but ideal.

Naomi encouraged her daughters-in-law to return to Moab

because she had nothing left to offer them. She was right, at least on a superficial level. She didn't have a family, wealth, or job opportunities waiting for her back home. There was no reason for Ruth or Orpah to leave behind the familiarity of Moab. But they didn't want to leave Naomi, so initially, they both insisted on accompanying her.

Notice the next verse. "At this they wept aloud again. Then Orpah kissed her mother-in-law goodbye, but Ruth clung to her" (Ruth 1:14).

Orpah chose familiarity. She said, "Okay, you go back, I'm staying here." That was the expected response, the logical one. Stay where everyone else is staying. Do what everyone else is doing.

But Ruth clung to Naomi.

That word "clung" suggests both passion and determination. Hold on to that thought. It's the first indication we get in this story that Ruth is not like everyone else, and the story just gets better from here. She was a unique, strong woman, and by the end of the story, God blessed her more than she could have ever expected.

Ruth has a lot to teach us about being single and secure. Let's look at four principles that stand out in her approach to life as a single person.

BE THE MINORITY BECAUSE THE MAJORITY IS OVERRATED

I already mentioned that Ruth held tight to Naomi, but that was only the beginning. Listen to the dramatic, impassioned speech that followed:

> But Ruth replied, "Don't urge me to leave you [illegible] back from you. Where you go I will go, and where you stay I will stay. Your people will be my people and your God my God. Where you die I will die, and there I will be buried. May the Lord deal with me, be it ever so severely, if even death separates you and me." When Naomi realized that Ruth was determined to go with her, she stopped urging her. (Ruth 1:16-18)

Ruth was outnumbered two to one: Naomi and Orpah thought it was best to return to her own homeland, but Ruth disagreed. So she stood her ground. Ruth was countercultural. She was strong and confident in her decision to choose her path, and her willingness to go against the majority opinion demonstrates an important principle:

Be the minority because the majority is overrated.

Ruth was determined. She was dramatic. She was ruthlessly Ruth. Even in the face of Naomi's insistence, even when her sister-in-law turned around and went back, Ruth didn't change her course. She knew what God wanted of her: to go back to Israel and to care for Naomi, no matter what might come. She chose right over easy.

Easy is what the crowd chooses. It's the path of least resistance, going with the flow, swimming downstream. But sometimes you need to go a different direction than the crowd. Why? Because you realize the importance of being who you are meant to be.

That's not easy, but here's what you have to remember. When you are yourself, you are in the minority. And when you are in the minority, you stand out. You get noticed.

A lot of singles say, "I cannot wait to meet the perfect person for me. I want that one-in-eight-billion type of love." Cool. But how is that person ever going to notice you if you look like

If you want to be single and secure, you're going to have to stop following the crowd. You have to quit living like the majority and instead be the minority.

minority.

everyone else? You have to stand out among eight billion people, and the best way to do that is to be yourself.

Just because people tell you that you have to dress a certain way to "catch a guy" or "catch a girl," or just because everyone else trades self-esteem and integrity for Instagram likes or social acceptance doesn't mean you have to. You get to choose the life you want to live. I'm not here to judge how you act, police how you dress, or criticize what you post on social media.

There is strength in opting for right over easy. In choosing to be you. In being secure enough to be who God created you to be and going where he is calling you to go.

Ruth is a powerful example of a single woman who knew who she was and wouldn't let anyone tell her differently. She understood what was right *for her,* and she wouldn't be dissuaded. Orpah had to find her own path. That's fine. But Ruth chose the direction she knew in her heart was right.

Ruth was not like everybody else. Neither are you.

Too many times, we give in to the value systems and philosophies of the world around us. We forsake our convictions out of convenience. We do what the crowd is doing, go where the crowd is going, talk like the crowd is talking.

But the crowd doesn't even have the life we want. So why are we following the crowd's advice? The crowd doesn't have an identity because everyone in the crowd acts the same. Why are we trying to imitate them?

If you want to be single and secure, you're going to have to stop following the crowd. You have to quit living like the majority and instead be the minority.

- Are you dating someone because it gives you status or makes you feel less lonely, but you know there's no way you could be with them long term? That's how the crowd treats dating.
- Are you in a relationship just to get what you can, even if you hurt the other person in the process? That's how

the crowd does relationships.

- Are you making choices about sex based on what feels good in the moment? That's how the crowd views sex.
- Are you hanging out with people you claim are friends, but you know it's all superficial and even toxic? That's how the crowd treats friendships.
- Are you making decisions out of fear or selfishness instead of love? That's how the crowd makes decisions.

I'm not saying the crowd is always wrong, but they certainly aren't as right as they claim to be. Sometimes, the crowd is outright stupid. You know that. You've seen it. And you recognize it because you're called to come out of the crowd. You're called to be counterculture.

You don't have to give in to pressure or conform to other people's standards. Be yourself. Stand out.

Be the minority because the majority is overrated.

STAY ON THE PATH BECAUSE YOU DON'T KNOW WHAT'S AHEAD

When it became clear that Ruth was not backing down, Naomi finally agreed to let her tag along: "So the two women went on until they came to Bethlehem. When they arrived in Bethlehem, the whole town was stirred because of them, and the women exclaimed, 'Can this be Naomi?'" (Ruth 1:19).

There's a little phrase in that verse that stands out: "went on." Naomi and Ruth didn't stay in Moab. They didn't stand by the side of the road, scared of the future, unable to make a decision. They didn't walk down the road for a while, then give up and turn back.

> They moved on.
> They moved forward.
> And ultimately, they moved up.

Here's the principle:

> *Stay on the path because you don't know what's ahead.*

Ruth and Naomi had no idea what the future held. Naomi thought she did, and it was a dark vision indeed: one of bitterness, loneliness, and poverty. She didn't have the luxury of reading the entire story in one sitting as you and I do because she was living it in real time, so Naomi assumed the worst. She wasn't being all that pessimistic, either—it was her reality. The reality she could see, anyway. But Naomi didn't know the plans that God had for her: plans to bless her, to protect her, to provide for her, to heal her heart and fill her with joy. How could she? She was only human.

Just like you and me.

Maybe you can relate to Naomi's bleak view of the future because, from where you stand, your future looks just as bleak. Remember, God is the initiator and the finisher of your faith and your journey. All he asks is that you put one foot in front of the other and keep moving, keep showing up, keep walking with him. Commit to God's way, then watch God make a way when there seems to be no way.

Success doesn't necessarily come to those who run the hardest, the smartest, the fastest. Success comes to those who run the longest. "Run" might even be too strong of a word. Maybe you jog. Or walk. Or crawl at times. Any of those efforts trump standing by the side of the road feeling sorry for yourself, watching life pass you by while you wonder when your turn will come.

st areas of life, the real key isn't speed, it's endurance. ... starting, it's finishing. It isn't lucky breaks, it's hard work.

You have to keep walking. Like Ruth and Naomi, you don't know what lies ahead because you're not God. He sees your whole life, your full story, all at once.

Just keep walking. Better days are ahead.

This principle of always moving forward is a crucial part of attracting the right marriage partner. Not that you need a partner to be complete, as I've said already and will say again. But if you desire romance and marriage, you need to be doing the things now that will make you attractive to the right person later. The strong, mature, visionary, healthy person you're waiting for isn't going to be drawn to your *potential* but to your *reality*.

Leadership guru and author John Maxwell writes about something he calls the Law of Magnetism, which he defines this way: "Who you are is who you attract."[5] He uses the term in leadership to describe leaders' tendency to gather people who share their values, attitudes, capacity, and skill level.

The same tends to be true for relationships. You've probably heard it before: like attracts like. You attract who you are, not what you want. Scary, I know. But it's true. People want to be with those who share not only their values, but also their momentum.

This is why camping out on the path can be just as detrimental as leaving the path or going backwards on the path. *Inaction* can be as unattractive as the *wrong* action. To put it another way, it isn't enough to not have negative qualities; you need to have positive ones. That is what gets the right kind of attention from the right kind of people.

If you're sitting by the road, doing nothing, waiting for your life partner to magically recognize you so you can skip hand in hand into your future, there's a good chance that person will skip right on past you. They won't want to wait for you to match their speed.

Get up. Get moving. Make the love of your life ca... you, not stop and wait for you.

You attract people who are like you because people have free will. They get to choose, and they aren't going to pick someone at odds with their values and priorities. It's okay if you have a list in your mind of the kind of person *you* want, but are you the person *they* would want? Love and attraction have to work both ways, after all.

> "I want a girl who's passionate, who knows what she wants out of life." But bro, if you're the most apathetic dude around, that girl you're imagining would be bored with you.
>
> "I want a guy with a great sense of humor, someone who loves life." Yet you mope around all day, complaining about everything. Do you think that's going to attract humor?
>
> "I want a girl who's ambitious." Man, you quit every job you start, and you play *Call of Duty* until four in the morning with the guys. Do you think that's going to attract ambition?
>
> "I want a man who's on fire for God." Yet you spend more time scrolling social media in one day than you do with God in a month, and the only things you pray about are finding a hairstylist to squeeze you in last minute or finding that little black dress in your size.
>
> "I want a good-looking girl, someone who takes care of herself." Dude, you haven't been to the gym in five years. Maybe you should be focusing on the man in the mirror right now.

I'm not being snarky or cynical here—I'm being real. What you are is what you attract. What you project is what you get. It's your decision.

BITTERNESS IS UGLY, BUT FAITHFULNESS IS ALWAYS ATTRACTIVE

Back to the story of Ruth. When the two women eventually arrived in Bethlehem, people started greeting Naomi by name, and it triggered her.

> "Don't call me Naomi," she told them. "Call me Mara, because the Almighty has made my life very bitter. I went away full, but the Lord has brought me back empty. Why call me Naomi? The Lord has afflicted me; the Almighty has brought misfortune upon me." (Ruth 1:20-21)

I don't speak Hebrew, and you probably don't either, but this was a play on words. A very cynical one. The name "Naomi" means "pleasant" in Hebrew, while "Mara" means "bitter." Naomi was saying that her life used to be pleasant, full, blessed. But then God took it all away, and now she's bitter and empty.

Ruth, on the other hand, was faithful. She was consistent and determined. She stayed close to Naomi and she kept her eyes on the future. Her choices illustrate another excellent principle about being single and secure:

> *Bitterness is ugly, but faithfulness is always attractive.*

Remember, the story of Ruth is not a tale of one single

woman, but three. Orpah opted out a long time ago. Naomi was present, but she was stuck in bitterness. While we can sympathize with Naomi's loss, and while there is a time for grief and mourning, bitterness was not God's long-term plan for either woman.

Fortunately, Ruth chose a different attitude than her mother-in-law. Their story is a study in contrasts.

> Naomi got bitter; Ruth got better.
> Naomi gave up; Ruth grew up.
> Naomi pushed people away; Ruth held people close.
> Naomi fixated on what she had lost; Ruth worked with what she had.
> Naomi saw God as her afflicter; Ruth saw God as her provider.
> Naomi saw defeat; Ruth saw potential.
> Naomi prepared for death; Ruth dreamed about new life.

Remember, the reason Elimelech and Naomi left Israel in the first place was because of a famine. Moab was an enemy of Israel, not an ally; it was a godless, pagan place, and Israel was supposed to reject it, not turn it into their home sweet home. This Israelite family had no business living there. That was *their* mistake, not God's.

God brought blessings out of mistakes, as he so often does. The young men found wives, and it appears that Naomi's daughters-in-law came to know the true God as a result. Ruth certainly did, and we can assume Orpah did as well. But it could have gone the other way. They could have pulled the young men into the idolatry of Moab.

In other words, Ruth is not a story of God letting down Naomi, but of God working with her mistakes and ultimately giving her incredible blessings. It's also a redemptive story because Ruth would not have ended up in Israel without Naomi. And by the way, many generations and centuries later, Jesus himself was counted among her descendants. Talk about God bringing good from evil.

Naomi was bitter because she didn't know what was ahead, but her bitterness was premature. *All* bitterness is premature. Why? Because just like Naomi and Ruth, your story isn't over until your life is over. If you're still breathing, there's still hope.

To be bitter is to pass judgment on past events. It means you label those things as wrong, bad, evil, hopeless, tragic—and final. And maybe they *were* terrible. I'm not minimizing what you might have suffered. But bitterness doesn't just recognize past hurt, it commemorates it. It builds a monument to it. It amplifies it. It drags it along with you. It allows the past to poison your present and sabotage your future.

Remember, God turns mourning into dancing and tears into joy (Psalm 30:11). He did precisely that for these two women, and he can do it for you. It's all in his time, though. You don't follow a God who works just in seconds or minutes or days; you follow a God who works in seasons. There are ebbs and flows. The great writer C.S. Lewis calls them peaks and troughs, mountaintops and valleys.[6] God takes you from one mountaintop to the next mountaintop, but the only way to get to the next peak is to go through a valley. Just because you're in a valley doesn't mean you should feel abandoned, condemned, or afraid. It's only a season, and all seasons come to an end.

If you're hoping to get married someday, it's to your advantage to deal with bitterness now because it's not going to do you any favors later. Resentment and hurt are not on anyone's list of ideal qualities in a spouse. Have you ever thought, *I want a man who is tall, dark, and bitter?* Or, *I'm dreaming about a girl who is smart, beautiful, and cynical?* Of course not. No one wants to fall in love with someone who is handcuffed to their past.

Naomi walked into town announcing her bitterness for all to hear, and I'm guessing it put a damper on the homecoming party. Sometimes we do the same thing: we talk about our hurt and hate everywhere we go. Not on purpose, and not always

Pain can be part of your story without controlling your story. You don't have to deny it, but you don't have to give it free reign either. First and foremost, *and* **you need to find healing and peace in God.**

with our mouths. Whatever is written on our hearts will be written on our face, though. It will come out in our words, our actions, our responses, our choices.

Bitterness is ugly. Bitterness deflects the blessing of God. It stiff-arms the opportunities God brings your way. If you walk around bitter for too long, you're going to deter the very thing you're asking God for, whether that is a spouse, a dream job, close friends, wider influence, or peace and joy.

I understand that the pain and loss you've experienced is real. Again, I'm not minimizing it. I'm not saying your hurt is your fault. Maybe someone wounded you. Maybe someone abused you verbally or even physically. Maybe someone cheated on you, abandoned you, betrayed you. If so, I am so sorry. That pain, that wound, is real, and you shouldn't ignore it.

Pain can be part of your story without controlling your story, though. You don't have to deny it, but you don't have to give it free reign either. First and foremost, you need to find healing and peace in God. But you might also need to seek therapy or counseling, or educate yourself in whatever area is broken, or seek justice, or push for reconciliation with someone, or set healthy boundaries. I can't tell you how to fix whatever has planted bitterness in you, but I can tell you not to water it until it grows and spreads beyond control. Bitterness is a weed that will choke the good things out of your life.

May I add something that might be hard to hear? The most important way to remove bitterness from your heart is to take control of your pain through forgiveness. I hope this sounds gentle, not callous: if you have gone through tragic, horrible things, the only way to fully release the bitterness is to forgive those who have caused you harm. I'm not saying you absolve them of wrongdoing or pretend the evil never happened. You can forgive and still hold people accountable, still call them out for their mistakes, still demand justice. This isn't about sweeping abuse under the rug in the name of forgiveness. Instead, it's about not allowing their betrayal to control you. Not letting bitterness poison your soul. That is not easy, and it's not immediate. But it will set you free.

Maybe you don't feel bitter against people, but against life itself or even God. That is where Naomi found herself. While it sounds odd to say, you have to forgive life, and you have to forgive God. Not that either of them is technically at fault, because life is not a person, and God doesn't do wrong. Grief quickly turns to anger and accusation, and maybe you need to release the bitterness you've held because things haven't turned out as you expected.

Maybe it's not what other people did, but rather something you did, and now you're struggling with regret and shame. Sometimes the hardest person to forgive is yourself. You have to let your mistakes go as well. Your past decisions do not define you. You are a child of God, and his grace is bigger than any error you could ever commit. You have to forgive yourself so that you can move into the future he has for you.

Whether you've held bitterness against other people, life, God, or yourself, there is a better way.

It's called faithfulness.

Ruth had also been hurt deeply, but she didn't change her name because of it. She didn't turn her loss into her identity. She simply remained faithful, and her faithfulness became the foundation for her future. She was:

Faithful to God.
Faithful to herself.
Faithful to her family.
Faithful to her values.
Faithful to her morals and integrity.
Faithful to her responsibility.
Faithful to her gifts and talents.
Faithful to her creative ideas.
Faithful to God's leading.

Faithful to the promptings of love.
Faithful to the future she envisioned.

Some people misunderstand the word faithful. They equate it with martyrdom or resignation, with giving up who you are to serve someone else.

That's not it at all.

Faithfulness is not being less of yourself but rather being *true* to yourself. It is the visible outworking of your invisible faith. It means living responsibly and diligently in the present because you know it will be worth it in the future. It's not about emotions or hype but about consistency. About perseverance. About integrity. About remaining true.

God rewards faithfulness.

And people do, too. It's attractive. It's magnetic. It's inspiring.

So, whether you're single, in a relationship, defining a relationship, questioning a relationship, or uninterested in a relationship, choose to be faithful.

Faithful to God.

Faithful to yourself.

Faithful to those around you.

Because faithfulness is always attractive.

WHEN YOU TURN UP, THINGS TURN OUT

Ruth's story was only beginning when she arrived back in Bethlehem with Naomi, but for the sake of simplicity, I'll summarize the rest of it. Ruth realized she needed to provide for the household, but neither she nor Naomi had jobs or income, and in that culture, widows with no financial support had very few options. But Ruth didn't let that keep her from taking advantage of the options she did have.

During grain harvest, poor people were allowed to follow behind the reapers and pick up any scattered stalks left behind. So Ruth did that. She was diligent, faithful, and hardworking, even though the conditions were less than glamorous. I can only imagine the frustration and humiliation she must have felt at times, not to mention the backbreaking nature of the work.

As luck would have it—and by luck, I mean God—she ended up in a field owned by a rich and unexpectedly kind bachelor named Boaz, who turned out to be a distant relative of Naomi. The Bible puts it this way: "So she went out, entered a field and began to glean behind the harvesters. As it turned out, she was working in a field belonging to Boaz, who was from the clan of Elimelek" (Ruth 2:3).

Notice that phrase, "As it turned out."

It's funny how often fortunate coincidences happen to faithful people. Author Coleman Cox famously said, "I am a great believer in luck. The harder I work, the more of it I seem to have."[7] This brings us to the fourth and final principle I'd like to show you from Ruth's story.

When you turn up, things turn out.

Often, success comes down to simply turning up. You can't control how things will turn out tomorrow, but you can show up today. And when you do, tomorrow has a way of taking care of itself.

I heard about a man who, decades ago, worked as a living mannequin in clothing stores. His job was to stand completely still as if he were an actual mannequin. He was good at it, and he was very committed to the role. Too good and too committed, perhaps, because one day a woman was arguing with her husband about whether the mannequin was real, and she ended up stabbing mannequin guy with a knife just to prove she was right. Which she wasn't, obviously. If I had been the mannequin, I think I would have said something before it escalated to that point, but maybe that's just me.

I don't know if that story is true or if it's an urban legend, but here's my point. Can people tell you're alive? Or are you standing so still that they are starting to wonder? My friend, if you don't want to be treated like an object, don't act inanimate.

Move.
Act.
Feel.
Decide.
Grow.
Become.
Risk.
Live.

Ruth knew when to act and how to show up, and Boaz quickly became captivated by her. Their courtship story is filled with cultural elements that are as odd to us as they are beautiful, many thousands of years later: his discrete but obvious flirtation, their growing romantic attraction, the vulnerability of falling in love, a plot twist in which another man seems about to ruin the whole thing, a midnight encounter in a lonely barn that is full of both innocence and sexual tension. It's like an ancient romance novel.

By the end of the story, Boaz and Ruth get married. They have children and grandchildren and, as I mentioned earlier, Ruth becomes part of the lineage of Jesus. An entire book of the Bible is even named after her. She has family, wealth, security, influence, and legacy.

Now compare the ending to the beginning. Remember, Ruth came from Moab, a pagan nation that didn't follow the God of Israel. She was a widow. She was childless. She was poor. She had a mother-in-law under her care. She didn't know anyone or have any connections. By all human reckoning, her situation was hopeless. In those early days after arriving in Israel, Ruth had three options:

> *She could give in.* She could resign herself to starvation or poverty, or she could return to Moab and leave Naomi to fend for herself.
>
> *She could sell out.* She could trade her identity or integrity for survival by turning to theft or prostitution or by manipulating her way into some sort of superficial success.
>
> *She could turn up.* She could work at whatever her hand found to do, making the most of every opportunity.

Ruth chose the third option. She turned up, and things turned out. She showed up, then Boaz showed up. She was faithful in her circumstances, terrible as they were, and God did the rest.

What if she had given up instead? She would have forfeited her future.

In any athletic competition, the worst way to lose is to forfeit. If that has ever happened to you, maybe in Little League or high school basketball, you know how frustrating it is. Perhaps the team was missing too many players, or the bus got lost on the way to the match, or the coach was stuck in traffic and never arrived. At some point, the refs had to call the game—before it even started. What a dumb way to lose. You didn't even get in the game. Didn't even try. Didn't swing the bat. Didn't throw a pass. Didn't shoot a basket.

That can happen in our lives, too. We can fail to turn up because we've been waiting too long or wounded too often. We don't turn up, so God has nothing to turn out in our life. Half the battle is just showing up.

It's not just important that you turn up; it's also important *where* you turn up. Ruth met Boaz in a field. She was working. She was making the most of what she had. She was taking practical steps toward a better future.

In other words, your environment matters.

Ruth put herself in the right place, and when Boaz saw her, it was clear to him that their values were aligned, even though their financial and social standings were worlds apart. Boaz then did some digging on her background, and he found out how faithful she had been to her mother-in-law. That sealed the deal for him. This was a solid woman, a secure woman. She was a go-getter.

Ruth was found because she was in the right environment, not because she was trying to be found. See the difference? She wasn't playing the field; she was working in the field. She was getting stuff done, because that's who she was. She knew what she wanted and needed, and she went for it.

Too often, people either want to play the whole field, manipulating everyone and committing to no one, or they want to avoid the field altogether because it's too much work or risk. And by "field," I don't just mean the dating scene, although it could include that. I mean the field of life. Of work. Of productivity. Of vision. Of responsibility.

What environment is best suited to your success? Where should you turn up, so things will be most likely to turn out? I'm not against clubs, but is that really where you want to meet your future spouse? I'm not against video games, but is that where you think your future career is? I'm not against hanging at the beach, but is that where you hope to make lifelong connections? Go to parties, play games, chill at the beach. Absolutely. But then, show up to work. Literally. And show up for church. And show up for class. And show up for your family. And show up for financial responsibility. And show up for your friends. And show up for your calling.

Sometimes great connections are made in social environments, so I'm not saying delete Tinder and incessantly scroll LinkedIn. But don't live on Tinder, either. If you want to build toward a stable future, if you want to find a spouse who is aligned with you, if you want business connections that work long term, you have to turn up where it really matters.

Want to be found by a special someone? Let them find you working. Let them find you building a future using what you have at hand because that's who you are. Strong. Resourceful. Motivated. Creative. Vibrant. Valuable. Secure.

Just keep turning up. Sooner or later, often in ways you didn't expect, things will turn out.

***

There is no right way to be single, and there is no normal way to do life. Whether you are just now becoming an adult, you've been a single adult for many years, or you're newly single, you get to choose your approach to whatever lies ahead.

Let Ruth, with her bold approach to singleness, be an inspiration—but make your own way because only you can decide how to live.

Be the minority.
Stay on the path.
Be faithful, not bitter.
And turn up.

That's all you can do, and it's enough because you aren't alone in this process. God himself is writing your story.

And it has a happy ending.

MANOUCHKA'S STORY

When I was younger, I remember wanting to be different so I would be noticed. I told myself that if only I could be "that girl," then he would see what he was missing out on. I was more concerned about how I was perceived than who I really was.

So, I had to wrestle with this question: am I trying to be someone I think the other person would like? Am I changing my likes and dislikes, how I dress, and who I am to impress another person? That's a slippery slope because, in the process, you lose a sense of who you really are. All your energy now has to go towards playing pretend.

I had to learn that standing out from the crowd also meant being truly myself. You'll often hear in church that God can't bless who you pretend to be. The same applies in relationships: you'll quickly find yourself unsatisfied if you aren't truly you.

Now, my focus is on becoming the best version of me that I can be. Being happy with me. Whoever I marry is going to have to love me for me. That's the person you want to be with—a person who allows you to be you, who gives you space to grow and become. Relationships are ever-evolving. We are ever-evolving.

Boaz knew everything about Ruth and loved her for it. He had heard about her past, and he wasn't intimidated by it. If someone can't handle all of who you are, that's okay. There will be someone who will. You don't have to settle or compromise. That's what I'm learning. You aren't meant to be with everybody; you are meant to be with somebody. So if everybody can't see or understand you, that's quite alright. You are not for everyone.

I'm not trying to get the attention of everybody. I'm going to be me, and who I am is going to be exactly what somebody needs.

CHRIS' STORY

Why does singleness tend to get a bad reputation? Being single should be exciting and full of life. The best decision someone can make in their season of singleness is to not make marriage the goal. Becoming the healthiest, best version of yourself should always be the goal.

My season of being single has revealed to me more that the non-negotiables are not all about appearances and personality, but they're about heart. It's so easy in today's world to scroll through social media and begin to dream up all the physical and emotional qualities of the person you desire to be with. I've learned this the hard way through past relationships.

As much as I can relate to Ruth's season of being single, I also relate to Boaz. My prayer is to be like Boaz. To be obedient enough to invite God into every aspect of my relationships. I can be single and secure because I know God is going before me. He is laying out the who and the what for me.

One of the worst things I can do during this season is to allow myself to become insecure about my singleness. Every day I have an opportunity to learn and grow. I won't allow myself to become complacent or comfortable with where I am on my journey. The last thing I'll ever do is settle for a life less than what God desires for me.

My season of singleness has served as a reminder that God has so much in store for me right here and right now. Following Jesus and having faith in the process is everything. I won't allow my mind to create unrealistic expectations that ultimately lead to a false reality. I'm committed to making my life less about my love story and more about His love story.

04 SECRETS OF SECURE PEOPLE

MY WIFE IS ONE OF THE MOST secure people I know. She's secure as a woman, as a mother, as a speaker, as a pastor—it's unbelievable.

I can't take any credit for that either, because when I met her, she was already secure. She knew her value. I had to work extra hard to convince her to even notice me precisely because she was so secure. Our conversations went something like this.

Me, smooth and suave: "Girl, you're incredible."

Her, cool and confident: "I know."

Me, confused because that should have had more of an effect: "Oh, well, you're amazing!"

Her, unfazed: "I already know that."

Me, stuttering a little: "You—you—you're beautiful!"

Her, checking her watch: "I already know that, too."

Me, exasperated: "How do you know all this?"

Her: "Because my dad told me."

Oh, my word, I'd think. There's nothing I can add here.

She already knew who she was. She didn't need me to elevate her, define her, or bolster her self-esteem, and that was a good thing because it meant she wasn't going to fall for empty words or flattery. Not that my words were empty—I was sincere and had good intentions. Mostly. But she was looking for a lot more than words and intentions. She understood her worth, so she knew she deserved a man who truly treasured and loved her.

While that didn't make my romantic goal easy to achieve, it made me value her more and pursue her even harder. I wanted to work to win her love. Why? Because when someone *knows* who they are, they attract people who *value* who they are.

Much of DawnCheré's security and value came from her father. He had told her who she was so often that she didn't have any doubts about her worth. He's a smart father. He set a high standard for the next man in her life.

Since she had an earthly father who was continually placing value and worth on her, when dudes did come around, their slick words couldn't divert her attention or sway her heart. She was looking for a man who would value and celebrate the woman she already knew she was. A man who would be willing to pursue her, earn her trust, and win her heart.

We've been married for over a decade now, so I must have been man enough for the challenge. Either that, or she felt sorry for me and cut me some slack. Probably a bit of both. Regardless, she is still an incredibly confident person, and I still pursue her every day.

You might not have grown up with a dad who spoke life and confidence into you. Parents often don't know how to raise their children in a healthy way, especially if they didn't have good examples in their own childhood. That doesn't excuse their mistakes, of course. It just means that you might have to address some traumas from the past.

We don't get to choose most of the early influencers in our life, but that doesn't mean we have to remain under their influence. We don't have to define ourselves by those voices, especially if they steal our value and undermine our security. It's sad how often, even decades later, we still hear the echoes of negative labels in our minds, and we give more weight to the lies than to the truth of God's Word.

Any of us can struggle with self-worth, and probably everyone does from time to time. Maybe you have "daddy issues" because you so longed for a father figure to place value on you: to say you're accepted, you're approved, you're beautiful, you're enough. Or maybe it's not daddy issues, but mommy issues. Or teacher issues. Or coach issues. You didn't have that strong figure speaking life over you. Instead, you had a voice (or many voices) speaking shame over you. And now, as an adult, you have a tough time valuing yourself the way you should.

The need for affirmation is legitimate, but please don't put the responsibility of supplying your missing confidence on anyone or anything else. It's too big of a burden for someone else to bear, and you'll end up disappointed again. No boyfriend or girlfriend can fix your self-worth. No career will magically give you confidence. No accomplishment could instantly infuse you with self-esteem. No pet could suddenly make you a secure person. (Especially cats, by the way—they'll give you an inferiority complex even if you didn't have one before. But I digress.)

Only God can change the way you see yourself. Well, God and *you,* because you choose whether or not to believe him. God is the ultimate father figure, and even if the past version of you was a jumble of negative labels invented by small-minded people, the future version of you can be defined by a God who sees you as he created you to be: inspiring, brilliant, and beautiful.

In the previous chapter, we saw how Ruth—unlike Orpah and Naomi—was able to process tragedy, embrace risk, and step into a future that turned out to have an almost fairy-tale ending. What enabled her to be so bold? What made her such a secure, confident single woman?

We could ask the same thing about people like the apostle Paul (who was single), John the Baptist (also probably single), and even Jesus himself (most definitely single). These biblical characters and others understood how to be single and secure. They found their value in something greater than smooth compliments or romantic attachments.

How did they do it?

Just like my wife, they understood their value—a value assigned by God—and this awareness gave them confidence, strength, peace, and wisdom. The Bible has a lot to say about this kind of security. Let's take a look at one of the best chapters ever written for single and secure people: Proverbs 31.

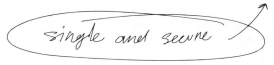

single and secure

PROVERBS 31 TEAM

Proverbs 31 is famous for its description of the "virtuous wife" or the "wife of noble character." It has often been misused to hold wives to an impossibly high standard while letting husbands off the hook. That was not the intent at all, and it's essential to understand what God is saying to us through this poetic passage written by a queen mother to her son. The son's name was King Lemuel. An unfortunate name, for sure, but the chapter itself is pure gold.

It's important to note that it was not written to a married person but rather to a single person. Why? I'm guessing the queen mother saw the girls her son was hanging out with and felt she needed to raise the bar. She wanted the most eligible bachelor in town to know what qualities to look for in a future mate. She probably didn't think anyone could be a good enough daughter-in-law for her son. And yet, I don't believe she was trying to set an impossibly high standard so much as she was trying to highlight for her son what really matters—especially since it's all too easy to get hung up on things that won't matter at all in five, ten, or twenty years. With the wisdom of age, she's telling her son—and all of us—to think differently.

That is not an indictment against someone who doesn't measure up perfectly, because no one ever could. Instead, it's a celebration of those who *do* demonstrate many of these qualities. In other words, don't hold yourself up to this list to see where you or a potential spouse are lacking. That would be an exercise in shame. Instead, look for these strengths and qualities when deciding if the two of you are on the same page. Do you value the same things? Are you going in the same direction? Do your skills complement each other? Do you trust each other? Do you work well together? Do you admire one another?

Note also that this chapter is written with both sexes in mind. Yes, the majority of the description is about the woman. That is due to the context: the queen mother had a son, not a daughter. I could point out multiple Bible passages that require men to hold themselves to the same standards mentioned by King Lemuel's mother.

The woman the queen has in mind for her son was not meant to be some trophy for his wall or an employee who would work under him. She would be one half of a beautiful marriage (the better half, I'm sure). In other words, the two of them needed to be a team.

If you haven't read the text recently, take a few minutes to do so now. Go ahead, I'll wait. As you read, don't just notice what the wife does—notice also what the husband must do and be in order to partner with and empower this strong, intelligent, effective woman.

He understands her.
He values her.
He needs her.
He listens to her.
He trusts her.
He respects her.
He celebrates her.
He releases her.
He validates her.
He encourages her to dream.
He lets her lead, work, and grow.
He trusts her judgment.
He wants her to succeed.
He acknowledges her contribution.
He models respect for his children.
He gives her the spotlight.

It takes two people to have this kind of relationship. She was an amazing woman with an amazing man by her side, and he was a strong man with a strong woman by his side. They were the original power couple.

By "amazing" and "strong," I don't just mean they were skilled at whatever occupations and activities they had, although that is part of it. They were *secure in who they were.* Proverbs 31 sets such a high bar that both spouses had to be secure or the relationship wouldn't have worked. One of them would have been jealous of the other, and it would have torpedoed their success.

If you want to marry a strong spouse, you'd better be a secure spouse. And if you want to be a secure spouse, you'd better start by being a secure single. It's that simple.

Before we jump into what Proverbs 31 says about singleness, spouses, and security, I've got three disclaimers. First, this passage is obviously about marriage, so we'll talk about the dating and marriage relationship quite a bit. That is not the only relationship that these principles apply to, though. If marriage is a long way off for you, or if you never plan to get married at all, these principles can still improve the quality of other relationships.

Second, it's worth noting how ahead of its time this passage is: rather than minimizing the importance of work in the home, it celebrates it. Instead of limiting the woman to the house, it portrays her as an entrepreneur, a businesswoman, a force for good. Far from relegating her to a gender-based role, it elevates her to be the person she was created to be and wanted to be. This is different for every person, every family, and even every stage of life, so it would be a mistake to read into this passage stereotypes about what a wife or husband should or shouldn't do. If anything, it's permission to think outside of stereotypes and to focus on a relationship defined by teamwork, not gender roles.

Third, these verses are directed at a single male looking for a wife, but they are equally applicable to both men and women,

If you want to marry a strong spouse, you'd better be a secure spouse. And if you want to be a secure spouse, you'd better start by being a secure single. It's that simple.

SIMPLE

as I said above, and to singles and married people. So if you're a guy, don't just stare longingly (or judgingly) at a massive list of qualities you hope to find in a spouse. Work on that same list in *yourself* while you wait, Lemuel, or your dream woman may walk by and keep going. And after you're married, don't assume the growth process is over and that you already won your prize: accept this chapter as a challenge and a goal to strive toward for the rest of your life. Power couples don't happen overnight.

Now, let's look at four secrets this beautiful and ancient text reveals about being a secure single—and how that security might be reflected in a future spouse.

DEMAND INCREASES WHEN SUPPLY DECREASES

The queen mother's description of the ideal spouse begins this way:

> A wife of noble character who can find?
> She is worth far more than rubies. (Proverbs 31:10)

Right from the beginning, the issue of worth comes up. Lemuel's mother is talking about the value of a "wife of noble character," but her wording reminds us of the importance we all have in God's eyes. He wants us to see ourselves as worth more than precious stones or anything else on this planet. He made us, and he is proud of his handiwork.

That's not empty rhetoric. You don't need to strive to be someone different than you are because you are who God created you to be. You just have to be the best version of you—the "noble character" version that God envisions when he thinks of you. To quote the psalmist, you are "fearfully and wonderfully made" (Psalm 139:14). The best thing you've got going for you is you. There is no one else on the planet like you. And because you are the only you, you are infinitely valuable. That brings us to the first secret of a secure person:

Demand increases when supply decreases.

That's an economic principle, which is why it makes sense to apply it to the idea of self-worth. Think about it: the less there is of something, the more it's worth. That is where the rubies mentioned in Proverbs 31 get their value. They are rare; therefore, they are valuable. But there are many more rubies than there are people like you, which means you are worth even more than rubies.

You are unique, irreplaceable, one of a kind. But only if you choose to be *fully you*, rather than lowering your standards (giving in) or lowering your expectations (giving up).`

You were created by the greatest artist of all. Quit criticizing God's work. Quit putting yourself down. Quit wishing you looked like someone else. Quit wishing you had someone else's life. Quit listening to the world's disdain. Quit wondering what people are whispering behind your back. Quit lowering your standards. Quit selling yourself short.

You might not feel worthy, so let me remind you of something. You are worthy for two reasons: because God made you and because Jesus redeemed you. Read the Proverbs 31 passage (and the rest of the Bible) with the understanding that God sees you as complete, not because of your accomplishments, but because you are his child and because Jesus has covered the price for any sin or error you might have committed.

Start listening to what God says about you. Why? Because if you don't see yourself as worthy, you'll treat yourself as worthless, and you'll let others treat you that way as well. But when you learn how valuable you are, you'll stop letting people cheapen you. There will always be moments in life when peo-

… your worth—just don't let it be *you* that can't see … r value. Don't discount what Jesus already paid full price for.

Note that what the text deems valuable is a person "of noble character." Character is your greatest asset, which is a relief because character is within your control. You can't change most of your physical traits, and you might have limitations in your finances, skill set, experience, or connections, but you can always improve your character.

There is no fast track to character, by the way. It is produced by two things: daily decisions and occasional trials. That is, *you build your character* by making good choices and building good habits day in and day out; and *character is built into you* as you persevere and grow through life's crazy challenges.

Neither of those things feels very exciting when they're happening. Making good daily decisions might feel boring or underwhelming, and trials and tribulations just hurt a lot. But you will appreciate the fruit they bring. I promise you. The apostle James put it this way:

> Consider it pure joy, my brothers and sisters, whenever you face trials of many kinds, because you know that the testing of your faith produces perseverance. Let perseverance finish its work so that you may be mature and complete, not lacking anything. (James 1:2-4)

While you might not appreciate character building while it's happening, you can trust that it is producing something worth more than rubies or gold: a healthy, secure, noble character.

Returning to Proverbs 31:10, note how the first line ends: "A wife of noble character who can find?" Another proverb says this: "He who finds a wife finds what is good" (Proverbs 18:22).

That idea of "finding" is key here. Why? Because finding implies a search, and searching implies that what is sought has value. Just because somebody wants you doesn't mean they value you, by the way. You have to be able to tell the difference. If they truly value you, they'll search for you until they find you. Again, think supply and demand. Be you. Be strong, courageous, and secure. The right person will be looking for you because the right person will value you.

This principle of supply and demand is also true for friendships, business partners, and other life relationships. Don't sell yourself short. Don't put yourself on clearance. Know who you are, and you'll attract people who value who you are.

On the flip side, make sure *you* are searching for what has value. Keep your eyes open. Don't become passive or apathetic. Don't surrender your future to luck or fate. If you value that future husband or wife, be on the lookout for them! They are rare, so it's only logical that the search might not be easy or quick. In any relationship of value, there will be an element of seeking and finding, of patience and perseverance—and that is especially true when it comes to finding a life partner.

Lemuel needed to know that finding this secure, noble, high-character spouse was not going to be easy. And that was a good thing. Because it meant he would search for her, and when he found her, he would value her. He wouldn't define her value, or lower her value, or ignore her value. Instead, he would celebrate her and empower her, and she would do the same for him.

If you're hoping to find a spouse in the near or distant future, learn to be yourself and to value people for who they truly are. Again, demand increases when supply decreases. Look for someone who appreciates you enough to pursue you, and be willing to pursue the person you value.

Obviously, there might be a few creeps along the way, so don't fall for the first person who writes you poetry. I think we all understand that, especially if we've been burned a few times. But there is also something to be said for noticing who really "gets" you, for who is pursuing you, and for being secure

On the flip side, make sure you are searching for what has value. Keep your eyes open. Don't become passive or apathetic. Don't surrender your future to luck or fate.

enough to open your heart up just a bit. It's always possible your King Lemuel or your Proverbs 31 queen is hiding in plain sight, and you've been too distracted looking for something you saw in a Disney movie to realize it. Being secure will help you avoid the creeps and value the royalty.

ADDING VALUE MAKES YOU MORE VALUABLE

As we've seen, demand increases when supply decreases: you are priceless because there is only one of you. Value goes both ways, though. A healthy relationship is not just about being valued but also about adding value. That is true in friendships, romantic relationships, work relationships, and family. Lemuel's mother put it this way:

> Her husband has full confidence in her
> and lacks nothing of value.
> She brings him good, not harm,
> all the days of her life.
> (Proverbs 31:11-12)

The second secret of secure people is this:

> *Adding value makes you more valuable.*

Secure people are always looking for moments and opportunities to add value to other people. On the other hand, selfishness sabotages relationships. You have to shift from a "get" mindset to a "give" mindset. Secure people tend to do this best because they aren't obsessed with getting affirmation from others, so they are free to focus on the needs around them.

Adding value can mean many things, and a lot depends on the unique relationship between you and your significant other. For example, giving encouragement, building self-esteem, contributing your time and talents, working hard, making sacrifices, forgiving quickly, listening, communicating well, and celebrating success can all add value to other people, but there are countless other ways to contribute to any relationship.

A healthy romance or friendship is one in which both parties give and receive. Receiving is easy, though. It's natural. You don't have to work at it or think about it. But giving requires intentionality and security.

Do you see your life as a gift? Are you a gift to your coworkers? Are you a gift to your friends? To your siblings and parents? To your boss? To your girlfriend or boyfriend or spouse?

You need to see yourself as a gift to others because that's how God sees you. You can leave any situation and any circumstance better than you found it. You can make every person you meet feel more loved, more valuable, more secure.

People are valuable, and one of the best parts of any human connection is being able to draw out, celebrate, and add to that value. Note the wording again: the husband "lacks nothing of value." In other words, he has what matters. He has what is essential. The verse is a bit vague, and that's on purpose because the point isn't what she gives him; the point is *her*. She is the value. She is the gift. She is the source of ever-increasing value in his life.

Again, don't lock yourself into gender roles here because this principle cannot work if it only goes one way. Both parties must be committed and capable of continually adding value to one another. Anyone who adds value to others is by definition valuable themselves, because they are a source of value. They create value. They speak value. They cultivate value. They are not just consumers; they are contributors.

Remember the old fable about the goose that laid golden

eggs? What was more valuable—the golden eggs or the goose? The moral of the story was that the source of a benefit is more valuable than the benefit itself. It's a gift that keeps on giving. Healthy relationships are that way. They aren't just about what we can offer each other, but about who we are.

The text also states that the husband has "full confidence in her." Why? Because adding value and building trust go together. Someone who adds value can be trusted, and someone who is trustworthy will add value.

How do you create trust? Trust comes through two things: *time* and *truth*. In other words, you build trust by being consistent and faithful over time, and you build it by being honest and authentic.

A relationship is only as healthy as it is consistent and honest. If you have to lie to each other, something is seriously wrong. You must be able to share what you feel and believe, and you must be able to trust that the other person will hear what you say, accept and love you regardless, and respond to you with the truth.

You can't fake that kind of relationship. When you have it, though, it's a beautiful thing. It's not always easy—the truth can hurt, and resolving conflicts is messy—but it's worth it. Secure people understand that adding value to others makes themselves more valuable as well and that building trust with people creates relationships that will stand the test of time.

TIME

TIME

TIME

time

WORRYING IS BETTING AGAINST GOD

The passage continues for a dozen verses that are full of poetic descriptions about how strong, secure, intelligent, and bold this woman is. The text then says:

> She is clothed with strength and dignity;
> she can laugh at the days to come.
> (Proverbs 31:25)

I love that image. Her strength and dignity are visible to everyone, and she is not afraid of what the future brings. Why? Because she is confident. Confident in God, yes, but also in herself. She knows she is prepared and diligent.

Those two things—belief in God and belief in yourself—should not be separated. They belong together. True faith means both trusting God *and* putting in the work because one will always lead to the other. This brings us to the third secret of secure people:

> *Worrying is betting against God.*

Worry assumes the worst about God's power, his intentions, and his will. When we live in fear of what might happen, we are essentially saying we don't trust God. We indicate we trust ourselves more than him, and since it's up to us, we're never going to make it.

Do you see the logic there? Or rather, the lack of logic? First, we cut God out of the picture; then, we give up on ourselves. Both halves of that sentence are wrong. We need to run to God, depend on God, trust in God—and then get up on our feet, go out into the world, and get things done. We are more than conquerors through Jesus, wrote the apostle Paul (Romans

8:37). Nothing can stop us from accomplishing God's plan for our lives.

Nothing, I would add, except fear.

You can't hide an attitude of fear. It leaks out. It shows up in your reactions, your words, your decisions. It sucks the confidence out of you. It says no to opportunities, it sees the worst in everyone, and it makes decisions based on worst-case scenarios. That is not the way Jesus lived, and it is not the way God has called you to live.

Worry is like faith in reverse. It's betting that the future will fail. Instead, you need to have faith that the future is safe in God's hands. You only get so much imagination. Why would you spend any of it on creating a world of negativity?

I'm not talking about strategic planning, which includes identifying potential risks or obstacles. Strategizing and planning are useful because they start from a place of positivity: you engage in them because you believe you can overcome the challenges you'll face. Worry, on the other hand, starts from a place of negativity, where problems take on a life of their own, thriving in some dark place in your head, and you have no hope of solving them.

> Planning is hopeful; worrying is discouraging.
> Planning plays offense; worrying plays defense.
> Planning is logical; worrying is emotional.
> Planning is objective; worrying is subjective.
> Planning is healthy; worrying is toxic.
> Planning attracts others; worrying repels them.
> Planning is excited about the future; worrying is scared of it.
> Planning believes God will be with you; worrying assumes he won't.
> Planning thinks about all scenarios; worrying fixates on the worst-case scenario.

The Proverbs 31 woman is meant to be an inspiration for each of us, single or married, male or female. She is strong, brave, and determined. You don't become strong by avoiding your fears. You become strong by facing your fears.

My mother is one of the strongest people I know. My dad was an itinerate preacher, and for twenty years, he traveled five days a week. During those years, my mother raised four boys, one of whom was disabled, mostly on her own and all while working a full-time job. Yet, she somehow managed to get us through school, take us to church every Sunday and Wednesday, and drive us to every athletic event. I can't think of a moment from my childhood when my mother was absent. She was a rock.

When my mom and my dad were in their late forties, they left behind their comfort zone in the Pacific Northwest, following a conviction and calling from God to move our entire family to Miami, Florida—where they didn't know a single soul—to lead an inner-city urban church. That took great courage and strength.

It's not that my mom was never afraid. I'm sure she felt fear at times. But she made a decision that worry would not be the culture of our home. She modeled that for us, she instilled that in us, and I am forever grateful.

My mom is "clothed with strength and dignity." You can't find that outfit at the mall. You can't walk into Bloomingdales and ask the salesperson for a skirt made from dignity or a jacket sewn out of strength. The only way you get clothed in strength and dignity is when you face your fears and declare, "I'm not backing down. I'm not running away. I'm not hiding. I'm moving forward."

The second half of that verse says she "can laugh at the days to come." The New Living Translation says it this way: "she laughs without fear of the future." That's an incredible attribute because one of the greatest fears we have is the fear of the future. Fear of the future is what causes us to worry.

Do you want the soundtrack of your life to be worry? Maybe you're single and you're thinking, *I don't think I'll ever get mar-*

imagination

Worry is like faith in reverse. It's betting that the future will fail. Instead, you need to have faith that the future is safe in God's hands. You only get so much imagination.

ried. I'm getting older. I'm twenty-five. I'm thirty. I'm thirty-five.

Then you get married, but worry doesn't go away. It just attaches itself to something else. *How are we going to pay our bills? Will we ever get a house? I've always wanted a house with a picket fence. If I had just one house with two bedrooms, I'd be so happy.*

Then you get a house, things are great, and worry goes away—for about five minutes. *What if we can't have kids? I know we'll never be able to have kids. I want kids so bad. I don't think I could live without them.*

You get kids, and they're adorable. Oh, wow! *How will I raise my kids? I'm going to be a terrible parent. I'm going to traumatize them. Oh no, he is throwing a temper tantrum in public! People are going to think I don't deserve to have children.*

But you get through those early years, and your kids love you, and they seem happy and stable. You've already started worrying about school, though. *How will they survive in elementary school? What if they don't have a good teacher? And what about junior high? That's so much worse. They might get bullied. And high school? What friends will they have? What if they get mixed up with the wrong crowd? How will they do on their SATs? There are too many tests. The education system is so messed up.*

They graduate. They even seem relatively healthy and untraumatized. But you're too busy worrying about college to notice. *What if their grades weren't good enough to get into the right college? What if they choose the wrong career? How will we pay for their schooling? What if they drop out? What if they start doing drugs? Will they ever graduate?*

They graduate! Oh, my goodness. *Will they ever move out of the house? They're never going to move out of the house. Or get married. I want grandkids already.*

It never stops. Do you want your life to consist of worry, worry, and more worry? You are not called to move from worry to worry, but from strength to strength, from grace to grace, from glory to glory.

The soundtrack of a secure person's life is *laughter*. Not because life is always funny, but because you have discovered that your joy doesn't come from circumstances and your happiness doesn't come from a risk-free life. The joy of the Lord is your strength (Nehemiah 8:10).

People are often afraid of the future because of pain from the past. They live from a wounded place, a hurting place, and they can't enjoy the present or laugh their way into the future because they haven't found healing from the past.

If that is you, I'm not making light out of all you've gone through. But don't allow something that should have been a difficult season to become the story of your life. This is a new chapter. Turn the page. That difficult chapter is still part of your story, but it's in the past, and your future will be better and brighter.

You can laugh at the future because God is already in your future. He has gone ahead of you, and he's making a way for you. You can also laugh at the future because you are strong, noble, and full of character. You are prepared and hardworking. You are courageous and committed. You understand how to love and be loved. You laugh a lot and worry little. You trust God and work hard. You are clothed with strength and dignity.

The future will not be perfect or easy, but it will be full of joy because you serve a God who gives you joy. Bet on God, not against him, and watch him take care of the days ahead.

Take care of
the DAYS ahead.

BEAUTY IS FLEETING, BUT JESUS IS LASTING

King Lemuel's mother closes her speech by addressing the same fixation with beauty and aging that we often deal with today. Apparently not much has changed in three thousand years. She says this:

> Charm is deceptive, and beauty is fleeting;
> but a woman who fears the Lord is to be praised. (Proverbs 31:30)

We live in a world obsessed with staying young, a world that equates beauty with youth. I suppose it's always been that way. The only difference is people used to believe in a magical fountain of youth, and today we believe in Botox.

There's nothing wrong with looking young. Staying fit and healthy is always a good idea, too. But I wonder how many people overlook one of the most beautiful badges of honor: age. Wrinkles are beautiful because every wrinkle is another line of wisdom. Grey hair tells people that you've seen much in life, that you have wise counsel to give.

The point of this verse is not just the experience that comes with age, but rather the importance of our walk with God. It tells us that if we focus on things as superficial as charm and beauty, we can end up neglecting what matters most: knowing and following God. That's what the phrase "fears the Lord" means in this context—not that we are paranoid or terrified, but that we are aware of God's presence, his reality, and his involvement in our lives. This awareness of God is what gives us security.

The fourth secret of secure people recognizes the importance of finding our identity and value in God, not in physical appearance:

Beauty is fleeting, but Jesus is lasting.

News flash: we're all dying. I realize that is not super encouraging, but we all know it's true. Dead cells are falling off your body right now. Maybe a few hairs, too. You can try to slow it, hide it, or deny it, but age happens and time marches on. When you look in the mirror and see a new wrinkle or when someone texts you a picture of what you looked like ten years ago, it should be a reality check and a reminder to invest in what will truly last.

What lasts? God does. He is eternal. No Botox needed. It stands to reason, then, that when we align ourselves with his will and design, we will find ourselves valuing and investing in things that last. We will build our lives on principles that outlast the temporary pursuits of this world.

Unfortunately, we often put more stock in the temporary than we do in the eternal. The last time I checked, the gospel is not a feel-good, look-good, cure-all for whatever ails you, but a deep inner force that changes you from the inside. Secure people understand that the power at work within them, and the walk with God that defines them, are more important than mere appearance.

Someone can look good on the outside and still be rotten at the core. You've probably bitten into an apple like that—it's such a disappointment. Charm can be deceptive and superficial. Beauty comes and goes. But a woman or man who trusts the Lord? They are to be praised. They are to be admired. They are to be sought after. Why? Because they understand what truly matters in life. They are even better on the inside than the outside.

That goes for you and me, and it goes for the people we invite into our lives. It goes for the spouse you might be praying for or the friends you long to have. Don't focus and fixate on the outside alone because a relationship with God is worth more than anything.

There are a lot of things about my wife that I find attractive. Maybe the greatest one, though, is that she is more in love with Jesus than she is with Rich Wilkerson, Jr. That gives me deep confidence because I know she is following God for herself, that she has her own relationship with him. God forbid, but if something happened to me, I know that the foundation of DawnCheré's life is the solid rock named Jesus. Yes, she would be sad (right, babe?), but she would rise up, and she would step into a future made secure by God because she's not completed by me. DawnCheré doesn't find security in a spouse. She finds security in a Savior.

Fear God. Don't be scared of him, but be in awe of him. Recognize his greatness and his nearness. Realize that he is with you, that he knows you, that he loves you, that he guides you. Don't be in awe of yourself or those around you, but be in awe of the God who created you. Connect your confidence to what is eternal: God's love for you. That's the only way to outlast the ups and downs of life.

We need a generation that isn't obsessed with self-image but rather with Jesus. The outward is fleeting, but Jesus is lasting. He's the only one who can fill your soul. He must be your first love and your greatest confidence.

If you've put too much hope in finding that perfect relationship, or if you've found yourself crushed because a friend betrayed you, I'd like to gently suggest that you turn to God instead. Rediscover Jesus. Find security in him. It's not a cliché; it's truth.

Maybe the perfect mate will walk into your life tomorrow. Maybe not. But regardless, you can be secure in your walk with God today. That is what matters most, and it is what makes the rest of life work. Beauty is fleeting, but Jesus is forever. And he's with you now.

***

Secure people value themselves because demand increases when supply decreases. Secure people know how to add value to others because adding value makes them more valuable.

Secure people laugh more and worry less because they know that worrying is betting against God, which is never a good idea. And secure people recognize that beauty is fleeting, but Jesus is forever.

How about you? Are there are any of these areas in which you need to grow a little? I need to improve in all four, and there's no shame in that. What if you chose one or two of these things and made focused progress on them this week? What would that look like, and how might that change you?

They are not difficult things to change, but they do require intentionality. You have to choose to live beyond the moment, to see further than yourself, to grow past where you are now. That starts with *you*, in *your head and heart*—which is the topic we're going to explore in the next chapter.

Secure people laugh more and worry less because they know that worrying is betting against God, which is never a good idea.

KAT'S STORY

"The first secret of a secure person: Demand increases when supply decreases. In other words, you are priceless because there is only one of you."

I didn't always feel this way. In fact, I grew up in a home where I wasn't taught about my value. I was made to feel "too fat" for my clothes or not pretty enough. Looking back, I now see that a lot of moments in my childhood and the words spoken over me led to deep-rooted insecurities in my teenage and young adult years. I never really knew what I wanted because I was so busy trying to look or act a certain way to find value and worth.

This bled into my relationships. I dated my first boyfriend on and off for several years, starting at the age of sixteen. He is the father of my beautiful daughter, Kassandra. I then dated another guy, and then another guy—each time not really sure what I wanted but trying to figure it out along the way.

It wasn't until I started attending church in my twenties that I began to learn about a God who not only loved me but had intentionally created me just the way I am. I learned that I was beautiful inside and out because He says so. As I got to know Him more and more, God spoke life and value over me in a way that has radically transformed my heart and mind from the inside out.

> *"I praise you because I am fearfully and wonderfully made; your works are wonderful, I know that full well." (Psalm 139:14)*

I learned that I am fearfully and wonderfully made. I began to love myself because of the talents and beauty God had created in me. I began to value my life and see the world through the lens of Jesus rather than through my insecurities. I learned to love others better, to invest in the relationships that already existed in my life, and to grow deeper and closer in my relationship with Jesus so that I could be confident not only in who I am but in what I would want in a life partner.

As I invested in friendships, I began to learn so much from my married friends. I learned that when two secure, confident people come together, it's a powerful and purposeful union. I learned to hold fast to my moral convictions and values above all else. I learned what I wasn't willing to compromise on. And most importantly, I learned to be complete in Christ rather than needing another person to make my life valuable, joyful, and exciting.

Being a single mom has also given me a greater sense of responsibility to model what it means to be secure and to know one's worth. I don't want my daughter to grow up in the same environment that I did, feeding deep-rooted insecurities. I am intentional to speak life and value over her and to choose wisely who I date and the way she sees me handle relationships.

In fact, just the other day, my daughter Kassy was writing a sermon (yes, she does that now—a true church kid!), and I found one of her "sticky statements" that melted my heart. She wrote, "God didn't put you on this earth just to add to the population, he put you on this earth because you have value."

I thank God for not only teaching me about my value but for being the rock and foundation of my daughter's heart and for speaking truth and purpose into our lives. If He chooses to bless me with a partner, I will be grateful, but I am even more thankful for the season I'm in right now and the lessons I've learned that have brought me to this place. Because of this season, I can be confident in knowing that the best is yet to come.

05 GET OUT OF YOUR HEAD

HEAD
head
Head.

BEFORE I GOT MARRIED, I was a relatively unselfish person—or so I assumed. But marriage has a way of highlighting self-centeredness you didn't know you had.

When you're living with someone around the clock, you discover that patience is harder than it seems, that humility doesn't come naturally, that your mouth often speaks without your permission, and that your partner has a couple of habits that grate on your nerves. Such as leaving the toothpaste cap sitting on the counter. Or finishing your sentences. Or hitting the snooze button six times. Or never leaving the house on time. Or taking your french fries even when she said she didn't want any. All of these are theoretical, of course, and any similarity to actual events is purely coincidental.

In our early years of marriage, DawnCheré and I had our share of arguments, discussions, and if-I-don't-tell-you-this-nobody-else-will moments. As a result, we grew closer and more united. We learned to walk together, to take each other into account, to rely on one another, to value the other person's feelings and needs, to forgive, to laugh at the small stuff, and to realize most stuff is small stuff.

Then we had kids.

When you have children, you discover how self-centered you *really* are. Why? Because parenting requires a deeper level of humility and patience than marriage. Your spouse, after all, is an adult. You can reason together. You can employ logic, communication, and emotional intelligence. Plus, you both bring a lot to the table—it's a partnership and you need each other, so there's a lot of give and take involved. And of course, you get to choose your spouse, so you go into the relationship voluntarily, knowing (or mostly knowing) what kind of personality you are marrying.

But kids? You don't get to pick them, for starters, so their personality is more of a luck-of-the-draw dynamic. Worse, there's no reasoning with toddlers, no rational communication—only primitive negotiation interspersed with desperate prayer and veiled threats and open bribes. And they bring nothing to the table (if you can get them to even sit at the table) except for needs and demands.

Take mealtime, for example. It's obvious they are hungry because they are having a nuclear meltdown, but they don't want the spaghetti you fixed for them. They want something else. Usually pizza. But of course, they didn't know they wanted pizza when you asked them earlier what they wanted—it wasn't until they saw the spaghetti on the plate in front of them that they realized they most definitely do not want spaghetti, that only pizza will satisfy them.

In moments like these, your self-centeredness often oozes like lava to the surface. Or it erupts, like a volcano you thought was extinct. How can these tiny creatures demand even more after all you've already done? Can't they see you are tired? Don't they care that you have needs too? Will this stage last forever? Who invented children, anyway? Does the local pizza place deliver? Important life questions.

I don't bring up any of this to scare you. The blessings and joys of parenting far outweigh the occasional temper tantrum (both yours and your kids'). I'm saying this because healthy relationships require you to *get outside of yourself*. Whether those relationships are with a loving spouse, a new baby, a best friend, a distant parent, or a complicated coworker, you have to look beyond yourself to sustain meaningful connections. In the previous chapter, we looked at several secrets to being a secure single, and those all start with this one choice to make your life about more than you.

You might as well start now. Don't wait until you're tracking down lost toothpaste caps or changing a baby's diaper to begin dealing with your human tendency toward selfishness. Work on becoming selfless starting today, in whatever season you find yourself. Learn to be less self-centered and more others-centered. Less caught up in your world and more interested in the world around you. Less focused on what you want and more focused on what you can give.

IT'S NOT ALL ABOUT YOU

Have you ever heard someone say, "I got in my head"? For example, they missed a critical free throw in a basketball game, or they blew a job interview, or they embarrassed themselves on a first date. After a good night's sleep and some painful self-analysis, they realize that the problem wasn't their lack of ability or character but simply that they overthought things. They got caught up in what could go wrong or in what people might think. Instead of focusing on the task at hand or the person in front of them, they focused on themselves.

That's always a recipe for disaster.

As humans, we tend to get in our heads way too much. We make everything about ourselves. We overthink things. We worry about what people are saying about us. We imagine all the possible bad outcomes of whatever we're doing and get stressed out before any of them even happen. We focus so much on ourselves that we lose the joy of the world around us, a world we are meant to explore, enjoy and serve.

We assume that the more we think about what we want or need, the better our lives will be. But the opposite is often true. Overthinking about ourselves is a distraction and an energy drain. It's not a healthy way to live, it doesn't produce happiness, and it won't help us reach our goals. And yet, it's hard to stop because we are so used to "centering" our needs, our goals, our fears, our dreams.

"Centering" yourself means making everything about you. Often, it involves looking at life through one or more of the following filters:

> What does this mean for me?
> What do I get out of this?
> What do I stand to lose from this?
> What makes me uncomfortable here?

How can I make my discomfort stop?
How can I use this to my advantage?

Those are not always bad questions, of course. You need to care for yourself. But that doesn't mean you have to make everything about you. We've all met people who do that, and it's not really a positive trait. Those are the people who often end up featured in the wrong kind of viral videos, throwing public temper tantrums about random things that shouldn't matter.

By the way, although we are talking primarily about self-centeredness in this chapter, the word "selfish" could be part of the conversation as well. Selfish and self-centered are related, but they are not the same thing. Selfish people see what other people need but choose to put their own needs first; self-centered people don't even notice other people's needs in the first place.

I'm not sure which is worse! If you have friends who fit in either of those categories, though, you already know that neither one is constructive in relationships. And yet, if we're honest, we probably all struggle with selfishness and self-centeredness at times.

To become less self-centered, we have to learn to become aware of other people's needs. To become less selfish, we have to elevate others' needs to the same level as our own so we can make wise, loving choices about how we treat people.

Neither of these steps should mean martyrdom, but they will require intentionality, humility, and generosity. Paul wrote this to the Philippian believers:

> Make my joy complete by being like-minded, having the same love, being one in spirit and of one mind. Do nothing out of selfish ambition or vain conceit. Rather, in humility value others above yourselves, not looking to your own interests but each of you to the interests of the others. (Philippians 2:2-4)

You were created to worship and live for God and to be part of a network of healthy, mutually edifying connections.

He was pointing out that we need to be intentional about noticing and caring for other people. God did not create you to worship yourself or even to live for yourself. That life philosophy won't make you happy long term, and it won't build the relationships you want. You were created to worship and live for God and to be part of a network of healthy, mutually edifying connections.

Being single should never be a justification for self-centeredness. Many of the single people I know are among the most selfless, generous, hardworking, visionary, loving team players around. That is awesome. These people are taking advantage of their season, not resenting their season. They are making their lives bigger than themselves now, and that will set them up for success in the seasons to come.

That doesn't happen by accident, though. These individuals have learned how to make their perspective and their world about more than just themselves. They have chosen to replace a self-centering mindset with a different way of thinking.

Paul referenced this change of thinking when he used terms such as "like-minded" and "one mind," and when he told the Philippians to "value others" and to look out not just for their interests, but "the interests of the others" as well. He wanted them to turn their thoughts outward, not inward. To get out of their heads and focus on the world around them.

So, how do you become a bigger person? How do you get outside your head? Although there's no one-and-done approach, there are four mindsets you can cultivate over time that will take you from self-centeredness to other-centeredness, from living inside the small world of your head to enjoying the vast world around you. When (or if) you get married or have kids, you'll probably still find a few dark corners of selfishness, but these four mindsets will help you to become a bigger person, and if you learn to integrate them into your social connections, they will help you navigate every stage of life. Even toothpaste battles and pizza wars.

SEE MORE THAN ~~YOURSELF~~

yourself

Have you ever tried to take a selfie in front of a famous landmark, but your head filled so much of the screen that the landmark was hardly visible in the shot? If so, you probably gave up at some point, turned around, and just took a picture of the scenery, without your big head blocking the view.

Something similar can happen in life. We can get in the way of the view. We can take up so much space in our mental frame that nothing else fits. Instead, we need to go from a selfie mindset to a scenery mindset, from a "look at me" attitude to a "look at that" attitude. The principle is:

See more than yourself.

To see more than yourself means you become aware of what is around you. It does not mean forgetting or neglecting yourself, but rather understanding *who* you are and *where* you are in relationship to the world around you. It's about awareness, context, and connection.

I love how pastor Rick Warren defines humility, which in many ways is the opposite of self-centeredness: "True humility is not thinking less of yourself. It is thinking of yourself less."[8] Humble people don't bad-mouth themselves or brag about themselves. They don't need to. They are secure. They know who they are, so they are free to think about other people, serve other people, and celebrate other people. They can see more than themselves.

Seeing beyond yourself requires two things: understanding your relationship with God and valuing your relationship to others. The apostle Paul wrote, "For none of us lives for ourselves alone, and none of us dies for ourselves alone" (Romans 14:7). If you read the context, Paul was talking about living for God, not for yourself. Then he expands that connection with God to include relationships with other people: "Let us therefore make every effort to do what leads to peace and to mutual edification" (Romans 14:19).

In other words, you don't exist in a vacuum. You are connected to God and you are connected to others. True humility and security come from grounding yourself in that dual reality. You might be single, but that doesn't mean you are independent. Don't make singleness about yourself any more than you would make marriage about yourself or parenting about yourself. You are always connected to others.

Seeing beyond yourself is the only way to make a difference in this world. In *Sandcastle Kings,* I wrote about an incident that happened a few years ago when I was completing my certification for scuba diving. Our class of about fifteen people was going to do a beach dive. We made our way into the ocean and were about to dive under when we suddenly saw a swimmer out in the water who was yelling and waving like a crazy man. We soon realized he was in danger of drowning. My instructor swam to him and brought him back to shore, and our whole group gathered around him as he caught his breath.

It was terrifying, but thankfully it ended well. The thing that struck me the most about it, though, was that throughout the incident, no one on the beach stopped what they were doing. People kept playing volleyball, throwing Frisbees, and putting on sunblock. Nobody noticed the danger. Nobody saw that a man nearby was on the verge of death. They were too focused on themselves to see what was happening around them, and a man almost drowned because of it.

We have to get our eyes off of ourselves. And we need to feel a sense of urgency about this, too, because there are people around us with urgent needs. Sometimes we are so fixated on our own immediate needs and personal goals that we don't notice what people around us are going through or how they are suffering. Those people matter to Jesus, and we are his hands and feet. They see and receive his love through us. Sure, improving ourselves is a worthy goal, but following Jesus isn't about becoming a better person, a better romantic partner, a better businessperson, or a better parent for our own sake. "Better" cannot be focused on self. Our lives must be about *people*.

Strive to be less selfish and less self-centered because *people matter.* Those around you need what you have to offer.

Look past yourself. See more than yourself.

The view is always better when your big head isn't taking up all the space in the frame.

DO MORE THAN YOU WANT

→ DO MORE THAN YOU WANT

Not only do big-minded people *see* beyond their immediate needs and feelings, but they also *act* beyond them. I'm not talking about a one-time act, but a lifestyle of others-focused actions, a habit of making choices based on what is right, not what feels good in the moment. In other words:

Do more than you want.

Getting out of your head means engaging with the world around you, even when that requires some work. Some discipline. Some self-control.

Have you ever been to a sporting event where they showed live, close-up shots of people in the stadium on the jumbotron? It usually happens during a timeout or at halftime. The camera pans across a random section of the stadium, highlighting people who may or may not be paying attention. It's so fun to watch because there is always that guy who doesn't know he's on camera, and he's just sitting there, bored and lazy. Then he catches a glimpse of himself on the jumbotron and something inside of him comes alive. He gets up and starts to dance like an idiot. He doesn't care what people think because he's up on the big screen and it's his moment to shine.

Society today sometimes feels like it operates on the jumbotron principle. So many people are okay with being disengaged while they wait for the camera to focus on them, for their lives to flash up on the big screen. The problem is that life doesn't work that way. You can't wait until your big moment before you engage with life. Lucky breaks are usually the result of years of hard work. Being discovered happens because you did the right thing anonymously for a long time, and finally, your talent was recognized.

You need to live every single day as if you were already on the jumbotron. And in a sense, you are—God is always watching. And you don't know who else might also be watching. Stay engaged. Keep moving. Keep building.

There is a misconception floating around in our culture that if you just do what you want to do today, you'll have the life you want for yourself tomorrow. That sounds great, but it doesn't work. The future you desire lies on the other side of some things you probably won't enjoy doing. That's just how it is. Throughout your life, you will have to exercise faithfulness and self-discipline—and it's worth it.

What is right to do rarely feels like what you want to do. I want to eat pizza every meal of the day. Maybe that's where my children get it. I don't do it, mostly because DawnCheré won't let me. And she's right. Eating pizza for breakfast, lunch, and dinner would not produce the result I want in my body or health. Heaven, though, is going to be streets of gold and DiGiorno pizza. You'll see.

You've been doing things you didn't want to do since you were a kid. You didn't want to brush your teeth when you were five, for example, but you're glad you have that habit now. Frequent visits to the dentist are expensive and sometimes painful.

It's a double whammy. Plus, chronic bad breath wouldn't help your dating life. So you keep brushing your teeth, day in and day out, morning and night, even though it's one of the most boring activities known to humankind.

You didn't want to do homework and take tests in elementary school. But you did, and now you can get a better job than if you were a third-grade dropout. Maybe you even went to college or grad school, which would have seemed ludicrous to your nine-year-old self. Who voluntarily goes to school? You do. Because at some point, you figured out that what you learn now will create a future with greater potential and freedom. So you study for exams and turn in papers on time, even without a parent threatening to ground you.

No one wants to go to work every single day, no matter how much they love their job.

No one wants to go to work every single day, no matter how much they love their job. But you can't quit just because it's hard. You know that. You need the paycheck. You need the experience. You need the connections and career growth. So you put in the time today to be where you want to be tomorrow. Working is hard, but it's easier than bankruptcy.

No one feels madly in love with their spouse every minute of the day. Sometimes marriage is difficult. But you can't walk out on your husband or wife when things get complicated. You're there for better or for worse, for richer or for poorer, in sickness and in health, no matter how long she takes to put on her make-up or how often he forgets to put down the toilet seat. And it's worth it. A million times over. Because those small daily decisions to set aside your own needs to serve your spouse build a level of trust and intimacy unlike any other relationship in life.

This principle of doing more than you feel like doing includes following God's way of life. For example, have you ever tried to apply literally what Jesus said in Matthew 5 about turning the other cheek? He said you shouldn't repay evil for evil or take revenge; but rather, if someone slaps you on one side of your face, let them whack the other side, too. And if someone wants to sue you for your coat, throw in your shirt as well. Or if they force you to walk a mile with them, walk two miles. That's where we get the phrases "turn the other cheek," "go the extra mile," and probably "give the shirt off your back."

Those are quaint sayings. They are easy to quote on Instagram. Until you try to live that way. For me, even if someone does something as minor as cutting me off in traffic, I want to speed in front of the guy and express my feelings in colorful ways. I'm not sure what I would do if anyone started slapping me around or stealing my clothing or making me go on forced marches. I doubt I'd react as selflessly as Jesus commanded in Matthew 5.

Sometimes, though, you can't truly understand God's truth until you obey it. Once you do it, once you walk through something, you discover the purpose on the other side. If you live according to principle and follow the path of wisdom, you'll reap the results.

Jesus told a famous parable in which he compared a wise man who followed his teachings to a man who built his house on a rock, and it withstood the winds, rain, and floods. But a foolish man, Jesus said, would not follow his teachings, and his life would be like a house built on sand, one that would crumble and fall in a storm.

In other words, if you do more than you want to do, if you live based on integrity, wisdom, and love rather than self-centeredness, you will build a solid foundation for your life that will enable you to withstand the storms. You can't control what lies ahead, but you can choose your actions and attitudes today. Don't trade what you want in the future for what you want now. Your job is to be faithful; God's job is to determine the outcome.

GIVE MORE THAN YOU HAVE

I have a personal trainer who is so good at what he does that I hate him. That's the sign of a great trainer, by the way. I don't hate him all the time, just when I'm working out. The rest of the time, I think he's an athletic genius, which is why I continue to let him put me through torture. I keep expecting this torture to give me a body like Jason Momoa. That hasn't happened yet, but a guy can dream.

Anyway, the trainer knows my limit, and he uses it against me. He always pushes me one step past that limit. I feel like that should qualify as some form of abuse.

"Rich, you've got more," he says.

"No, I don't," I groan, "I really, really don't."

"Come on, you've got one more in you."

"I swear to you, I don't. I don't have half of one more in me."

"You do, come on, let's go. One more."

I've learned that when I trust my trainer, when I dig deep, I find strength for one more. And that's where my greatest increase of strength and stamina come from: those moments when I thought I had given it all, but I still had a little more inside. And that's the mindset of big-minded people:

Give more than you have.

In other words, dig deeper than you think you can, and give more than you thought you could spare. If you want to get stronger, you have to go harder. If you want to carry more, you have to get under more. If you want to grow a lot, you have to groan at least a little bit. It's the pressure that produces the power.

There will be moments when you say, "I don't have any more to give."

God will say, "Yes, you do."

And if you can trust your trainer, if you can dig deep, you'll find the strength to give a little more. That is where you'll grow the most. It's where you'll discover the depth of potential that God has given you.

Now, there is a limit to your strength, and that's where God steps in with his grace to do more than you could ever do on your own. This is where the analogy breaks down a little because my trainer encourages me, spots me, tortures me, and believes in me, but he doesn't carry any weight. That's not his job.

God, however, works alongside us, with us, through us, and even in spite of us. He is more than a coach and a trainer. He is our strength. He is our strong tower. He is our mighty Savior.

Maybe you've heard the phrase, "God won't give you more than you can handle." I know what people mean by that, but I've found it to be untrue. Many times in my life, God has allowed pressures that I haven't been able to handle. Challenges that drove me to my knees. And sometimes when I said, "Lord, I don't have even one more," he replied, "That's okay. I do."

The apostle Paul told the Corinthian church that, on three different occasions, he cried out to God about a particular weakness he faced. God replied, "My grace is sufficient for you, for my power is made perfect in weakness" (2 Corinthians 12:9). Paul wasn't enough, but God was.

That same principle is at work in you and me today. You have to believe it, and you have to respond to the voice of God saying, "You can do one more. You can go a little longer. You can give a little more."

The word "sufficient" means adequate for its purpose. It means just the right amount. God's grace in your life is precisely what you need for your purpose. Not for someone else's purpose, but for *your* purpose—for who God created you to be. Don't try to be someone else and don't stop short of being yourself.

God's purpose for your life will require you to give more than you think you can. I'm not talking about money, although financial generosity is part of what you can give, and it is undoubtedly a reflection of your faith. I'm talking about giving everything. About leaving it all on the court. You can't take anything to heaven, so you might as well use your life to its fullest here on earth.

There's a great line in Proverbs that says, "The world of the generous gets larger and larger; the world of the stingy gets smaller and smaller" (Proverbs 11:24 MSG). That means that the more we give, the bigger our world gets. We often think that the key to success and stability is holding on to what we have, getting more for ourselves, and doing what we want. We say, "If I collect these things, if I hold tightly to what I have, my world will get bigger."

No, it won't.

The gospel of Jesus teaches us that giving is better than receiving. That serving is the path to greatness. That dying to self is the only pathway to a full, abundant life. The principle of sowing and reaping is found throughout the Bible: if you want to grow in an area, you have to sow in that area.

> If you want friends, be friendly.
> If you want financial blessing, be generous.
> If you want to be loved, learn to love unconditionally.
> If you want peace, be a peacemaker.
> If you want respect, earn it over the long haul.
> If you want responsibility, be faithful in the small things.
> If you want joy, choose to focus on the positives.
> If you want people to listen to you, listen to them.
> If you want health, take care of your body.
> If you want your own french fries, don't get married.

Until we see more than ourselves, do more than we want, and give more than we have, we won't walk into a bigger world. Our world will get smaller and smaller until we are the only ones who fit in it. What a lonely way to live! But the opposite, a world that gets bigger and bigger? That sounds incredible.

It's your choice. Will you give a little bit more than you think you have, day in, day out? If so, while I can't promise you a body like Jason Momoa, you will have a heart like Jesus. That's even better.

LOVE MORE THAN YOU FEEL

The apostle Paul wrote, "Keep your eyes open, hold tight to your convictions, give it all you've got, be resolute, and love without stopping" (1 Corinthians 16:13-14 MSG). What was he saying? That love is a choice we make. It is not predicated on a feeling but rather on a decision. The fourth and final mindset of big-minded people is this:

Love more than you feel.

Love includes feelings, but it goes beyond them. True love is a choice to give selflessly, continually, and unconditionally. It doesn't wait for feelings to line up before it acts. It tells the feelings themselves how to act.

Here's the thing, though. Everyone loves the idea of love, but not everyone loves the sacrifice love requires. The two must go together, though, or it's not love at all. Love has a price. Love leaves a mark. That's exactly why it is so powerful.

I love being married, and I love being a parent. I wouldn't change either for the world. There are some things I miss about being single, though. When you're single, you own everything in your house, for example; you get to decorate the whole place how you want. When I married DawnCheré, nobody prepared me for this little detail. I had a beautiful art piece hanging on my wall. It was a Michael Jordan Wings poster. On the first day of our life together, she was like, "Rich, this has to go."

"That is a work of art," I said, "What are you talking about?"

"No, it's not. Take it down."

"Girl, you don't know good art when you see it!" Then I took it down.

When you're single, you control everything in your bank account. The only debt you have is yours. You can make all the dumb impulse purchases you want and nobody says anything. You know what you have and you know what you can spend. Life is simple. Then you get married, and suddenly you don't recognize all the purchases on the bank statement. Now two people are making dumb impulse purchases. That's when the poetic ideas that "love has a price" and that "love will cost you something" become way more practical than you imagined before you got married.

When you're single and you go to a restaurant, your entire meal is yours. But when there's a significant other in your life? She looks at your food and says, "Wow, that looks good!" And you know it's over. Even your food is shared now.

Don't even get me started on parenting. You think you're busy now? You think you're tired now? (Cue maniacal laughter.) Just wait until you have kids, my friend.

Would I have it any other way? Would I change anything? Would I go back to being single or not having children?

Absolutely not.

Love includes responsibility, sacrifice, hard work, mutual submission, and dying to self. And it is so worth it. Not just in marriage and family, either, but in every relationship.

Yes, we might have to adjust to differences in our decorating taste, our budgeting, our schedules, or a million other things. Those pale in comparison to a life shared with a wife, husband, children, close friends, or extended family, though. They don't even feel like sacrifices because love has a way of uniting not just our hearts but our habits. We realize that we would rather walk together than alone, and the adjustments of walking together are worth the hard conversations and the occasional sacrifice. The benefits of love far outweigh the costs of love.

Love is willing to give because love is others-centered. That is the very nature and definition of love. It is expansive; it is generous; it is selfless. Even when we don't "feel" like loving that way, true love is the greatest motivator, the strongest emotion, and the most irresistible force. Love wins out over feelings.

I am thankful Jesus loved me even when he was being nailed to a cross. He didn't say, "This doesn't feel like love. This hurts too much." He loved us to death, literally. He loved us even when it hurt, and he bore on his body the marks of his selflessness.

Real love always leaves a mark, as I said before. That's not a bad thing. It's the proof of love, the badge of love, the power of love. If you want a united marriage, guess what? You'll have to go through some difficult moments. If you are going to love your children, there will be times when you just hang on, giving your

Even when we don't "feel" like loving that way, true love is the greatest motivator, the strongest emotion, and the most irresistible force. Love wins out over feelings.

all, sacrificing your comfort and your preferences for the good of your family. If you plan to fulfill a dream God gave you, maybe in business or ministry, there will be a price to pay. You won't get through the process without some battle scars.

Embrace that reality. Expect it. Prepare for it. I'm telling you, it will be worth it.

The Bible embraces the idea that love comes with a cost. The Old Testament book named Song of Solomon is a collection of poems that celebrate romantic love between King Solomon and a woman known only as the Shulamite. Listen to these words, spoken by the Shulamite:

> Place me like a seal over your heart,
> like a seal on your arm;
> for love is as strong as death,
> its jealousy unyielding as the grave.
> It burns like blazing fire,
> like a mighty flame.
> Many waters cannot quench love;
> rivers cannot sweep it away.
> If one were to give
> all the wealth of one's house for love,
> it would be utterly scorned.
> (Song of Solomon 8:6-7)

Her passion and desire are clear, but there is also a depth of commitment beyond momentary emotion. Love is "as strong as death." It "burns like blazing fire." "Many waters cannot quench love." And all the wealth one could possess is "utterly scorned" in comparison to love.

Don't fall for the myth that true love will always feel easy. Sometimes you work at it. Sometimes it burns a little. Sometimes you have to hang onto love for dear life when the waters of life threaten to drown you both. That's not a negative: as both of you work on your relationship, as you walk together through the process of becoming one, your love will grow stronger than ever.

This process doesn't taint love, it beautifies it.

While this poem addresses romantic love, the same principle of "loving more than you feel" is true for other relationships in your life. People matter more than anything else in this life. Get good at loving people, even those who are a little harder to love than others. Learn what it means to love like Jesus.

I understand there are times when we have to draw lines and establish boundaries. Again, loving well isn't about martyrdom or enabling dysfunction. True love will empower you to have those difficult conversations and to make hard choices. But if the people in your world are the ones you should be investing in and doing life with, decide to make a lifestyle out of loving more than you feel. Sooner or later, feelings catch up with decisions.

You'll never regret the choice to love.

***

A life lived for others is the best kind of life. And ironically, it's the most fulfilled life, too. It's that paradox of faith: the more you love and serve others, the more abundant your life becomes.

Regardless of what season of life you find yourself in, get out of your head. Take the time and put in the work to:

See more than yourself.
Do more than you want.
Give more than you have.
Love more than you feel.

Your world will get bigger, your relationships will be stronger, and your heart will be fuller. And hey, you can always order an extra side of fries.

JOSHUA'S STORY

Relationships are the most precious, joyful, and meaningful possessions in my life. They are also some of the scariest, difficult, and challenging. I am thirty-four years old now, and if I have learned one thing in my journey, it's that I need to get out of my head…and out of my own way!

I recall a moment when I spent some time praying specifically over my "relationship status," and God gently reminded me, for the trillionth time, that I'm called to trust and honor him where I am and with what I have. As I thought about my previous relationships, I found that many of them lacked vulnerability, which hurt the quality and success of the relationship.

Apprehension of vulnerability is a trust problem and a selfishness problem. It communicated three things about me. First, that I didn't trust God with the person he had brought into my life and that I didn't trust the person with me. Secondly, it showed that I was far too focused on me. On my feelings, my fears, my insecurities, and my limited understanding. Though I would never have admitted it then, my selfishness ultimately prevented me from being in a place where I could communicate freely, be known, and be loved. Third, it showed me that when it came to relationships, I was too myopic. I was focused on the here and now feeling or my understanding of it all. The easiest way for me to stop focusing on myself was to focus on others!

Our God works his perfect plans out over time, and I have a responsibility to be faithful at building healthy practices now. To work on the hard stuff now and be faithful where I'm at. Hard stuff like: (1) making sure first things are first in my relationship with Jesus, (2) being intentional about cultivating meaningful time with family, (3) ensuring I have accountability and mentorship with a solid group of guys around me, (4) committing to serving my local church and community, and (5) being diligent in occupation and physical fitness. Ultimately, what I do in the small things is what I will do in all things.

I have learned that the best way to win in relationships is to get comfortable with being vulnerable and trusting God with my "self." I want to be faithful in the here and now, regardless of my relationship status. There's so much to be done, experienced, and enjoyed in life. Being focused on self is way too small of a world.

As a single person, I still have many relationships, so it's a gift and opportunity that I get to work on developing healthy relationship habits now: at work, with family, with friends, at church, in the gym, with my neighbors, and more. I look forward to forming a lifelong relationship with my someone special and enjoying a forever type of companionship someday. But between now and then, I'm giving everything to honor God where I'm at with and with what I have.

what I have.

06 A SEASON FOR EVERY- THING

season

MAKING NEW YEAR'S RESOLUTIONS has to be one of the most human things we do. I can't imagine any other species taking the time once a year to make promises to themselves that they never intend to keep.

Gyms plan on this phenomenon, of course. They know two things: that most people wish they were in better shape, and that those who sign up for a new gym membership in January will stop showing up after a month. So the gyms run end-of-the-year and beginning-of-the-year promotions convincing people to pay six months or a full year in advance. If you're a regular gym-goer, you probably understand this phenomenon already, and you avoid the gym in January because it will be full of zealous, sweating newbies—but you know that by February, things will be back to normal.

I'm not knocking self-improvement goals here. And I'm as guilty as anyone of making resolutions I can't keep. The act of making a list feels like an accomplishment in itself, though, which is probably why we do it. And we are eternally optimistic about the future version of ourselves, which is a good thing, even if it means we won't cancel that recurring monthly gym payment because we are convinced that starting next month we're going to be there every single day at six in the morning.

"Get in shape" is undoubtedly one of the most common New Year's resolutions, but there are many more you might have tried.

Pay off debt.
Spend more time with family and friends.
Reduce stress.
Travel to new places.
Read more books.
Get more sleep.
Date more.
Date less.
Learn a new language or hobby.
Finish a home repair project.

> Start a TikTok account for your pet lizard.
> Learn to juggle chainsaws.
> Study quantum physics.
> Raise llamas and learn to knit their wool.

You probably share some of these goals or have a few of your own, and that's great. Setting goals and starting new things are necessary parts of life.

Remember this, though: you don't just need a list of things to start—you need a list of things to *stop*. You can't keep adding new activities or goals indefinitely, because you are finite. In order for something to begin, something else often has to end.

For example, if you want to get in shape, then yes, a gym membership is a good idea. But unless you pair that with eating less junk food, you won't see the results you expect. You need to start exercising *and* stop eating unnecessary calories. Success isn't just about starting the right things; it's also about stopping the wrong ones.

Jesus acknowledged this principle in a conversation with his disciples:

> I am the true vine, and my Father is the gardener. He cuts off every branch in me that bears no fruit, while every branch that does bear fruit he prunes so that it will be even more fruitful. (John 15:1-2)

He used the metaphor of pruning to explain that sometimes God will remove certain things from our lives that are either harming us or distracting us.

If you've ever watched an arborist prune a fruit tree, you know that pruning is savage. When the pruning is done, the ground around the tree looks like a tornado tore through the area. Anyone who didn't understand pruning would look at the leafy carnage and wonder, *Why are you getting rid of those perfectly healthy branches?*

But the arborist knows that the tree doesn't have an unlimited supply of nutrients, and some foliage must be removed so nutrients can reach the branches that matter most—the ones that produce fruit. If the tree isn't pruned, eventually, none of the branches will bear fruit because they'll all be struggling just to stay alive.

Here's the principle: *If you aren't pruned in life, you won't produce in life.* In order to grow, you have to leave a few things behind. You must get rid of what is not productive so that what remains can bear more fruit. Often, that pruning process happens naturally, as God brings changes to your life. Other times, you have to actively decide to make changes.

The things that are pruned might not be evil in themselves, but they can simply be distracting you or diverting resources from areas that could be bearing more fruit. They might include:

- Anxiety, fear, or other internal energy drainers
- Toxic or distracting relationships
- Overly consuming hobbies
- Addictions
- Activities that hurt your conscience
- Emotionally draining conversations, conflicts, or people
- Wrong romantic relationships
- Overcommitment
- A dead-end job
- Unhealthy ways of responding to stress
- Immaturity or childish ways of living

Only you can know what you need to start and stop because *this is your life.* No one else has the insight you do into yourself, and no one else has the responsibility to change you.

Again, the things that are being pruned might not be wrong in themselves, but they are wrong for *you at this point in time.* You are going in a different direction now. You're not the same person you used to be. And you need to let some branches be cut off.

That sounds great in theory. But pruning feels a lot like a tornado tearing through your life. And when you lose a few things that you never imagined living without, when branches and leaves are strewn everywhere, it can be hard to believe those things were getting in the way of sustained growth. You might even want to shove them back on the tree somehow because you miss the good old days.

Before you attempt to fix what seems to be breaking, before you try to hold on desperately to whatever is falling away, and before you refuse to move on, ask yourself if maybe God is cutting off the things that are holding back your growth. Instead of looking at the ground in dismay, look at the buds on the tree. There is greater fruit in your future.

SEASONS COME, SEASONS GO

Pruning is preparation for a growth season, according to both Jesus and arborists. There are times for pruning, trimming, and scaling back, and there are times for blossoming, productivity, and growth. Same life, different seasons. You need to pay attention to the season you are experiencing.

This concept of changing seasons is found many times in Scripture, and it's a helpful principle to understand. In life, just as with the weather, seasons come and seasons go. Each one brings its own opportunities, challenges, and needs. King Solomon, the wisest man who ever lived, wrote this:

> There is a time for everything,
> and a season for every activity under the heavens:
> a time to be born and a time to die,
> a time to plant and a time to uproot,

> a time to kill and a time to heal,
> a time to tear down and a time to build.
> (Ecclesiastes 3:1-3)

I'm quoting just three verses here, but he goes on for five more, listing a wide variety of seasons and reminding us that there is a time for everything.

Those changing times can feel contradictory. That's part of the point. One day you're planting, the next you're uprooting. One day you're crying, the next day you're laughing. One day you're pruning, the next day you're blossoming.

That's okay. It's called life.

The challenge is that we often don't get to choose our season. And just when we get used to one season, a new season begins. That can make us feel afraid and out of control, so we try to cling to something that is no longer bearing fruit.

Resist that temptation. Embrace new seasons. Learn to welcome change. Navigating change without losing your mind is an essential life skill.

For example, consider Uber. I love Uber. This little app can get me a ride to anywhere I want to go within minutes. It's easy, it's intuitive, and I use it all the time. Uber has changed the transportation game.

Do you know who doesn't love Uber? Taxi drivers. The taxi industry can't keep up with change. They are fighting a lost cause, though, because the season has shifted. Taxi drivers can complain and holler all they want, but times have changed. Rather than fighting for taxi cabs, they should sign up for Uber and decide, "I'm going to be the best Uber driver the world has ever seen."

Or look at Netflix. A couple of decades ago, who would have thought that massive chains like Blockbuster would go bankrupt because an upstart video company named Netflix was mailing DVDs to people via snail mail and—almost inconceivably—abolishing late fees? Then, once broadband internet became more common, they started streaming movies *over the*

Internet from a massive online catalog. That was the stuff of sci-fi movies back then. Meanwhile, big video rental stores were still operating on the old model, where you had to drive to their stores, pick out a movie from whatever random DVDs they had in stock at the moment, pay late fees (because you never returned movies on time), and then drive home—by which time your family had fallen asleep or pulled out a board game. Then Netflix started creating its own content, upending the way movies are made, distributed, and viewed. The entire television and movie industries have had to shift to accommodate the reality that consumers want to control what they watch and when they watch it without having to drive to a movie rental store (and pay late fees).

The examples are endless. Think about Airbnb cutting into the hotel industry. Or Amazon dominating the retail shopping space. Or Expedia and other travel services replacing travel agencies. Or print-on-demand publishing turning the book industry upside down. Or online education opening up new learning horizons for millions of people. Or the constantly shifting world of social media platforms. Or how online dating apps have forever changed the world of relationships. Or the rise of Zoom thanks to a worldwide pandemic.

I could go on, but the point is this: you either change or die. You either read the season and respond to the season, or the world moves on without you.

> You are changing.
> Your friends are changing.
> Your significant other is changing.
> Your parents are changing.
> Culture is changing.
> Church is changing.
> Technology is changing.
> Education is changing.
> Careers are changing. → *changing*

Don't fight every change. Don't hold on to the branches that aren't bearing fruit. Recognize the changing seasons, respond to them, and enjoy them. Growth is coming, but it is on the other side of change, and change means letting go of a few things.

Maybe right now, you're going through a difficult season, or a boring one, or a frustrating one, or a contradictory one. Or maybe not—it could be that you're experiencing more fruit than ever before and pruning is the last thing on your mind. Wherever you are at today, the only thing you can guarantee is that change is coming. It could be tomorrow, next month, or maybe next year. You can't know for sure, but it's coming, and that's a good thing.

The real goal, then, is learning to manage change. How do you embrace new seasons? How do you embrace the pruning so the fruit can come? Let's look at four principles for navigating the changing seasons of life—don't waste the waiting, water your own lawn, find your light, and honor and enjoy the season.

A WAITING SEASON DOES NOT HAVE TO BE A WASTED SEASON

The first principle to understand when it comes to seasons of life—especially the tough ones—is this:

A waiting season does not have to be a wasted season.

As author and pastor Craig Groeschel once put it, "A waiting season is never a wasted season. Sometimes God may want to do something *in* you before he does something *for* you."[9]

I would add that in addition to doing something in you,

God might also be doing something in your future spouse, in the economy, in your workplace, in your children, or in a million other places. God is always at work; we just don't see it most of the time. Even though it might seem like things aren't changing on the outside, God is still moving his plans forward. He hasn't given up on you or forgotten about you. The psalmist describes God's constant attention toward you:

> He will not let your foot slip—
> he who watches over you will not slumber;
> indeed, he who watches over Israel
> will neither slumber nor sleep. (Psalm 121:3-4)

In other words, God is always paying attention and always working, usually in multiple areas of your life at once. He is the ultimate multitasker.

The problem is that we tend to focus only on what we can see—and what we can see barely scratches the surface of what is actually happening. We want to see change occur in real time, and we assume that if the change isn't visible, nothing is happening. But we are surrounded by things that take place gradually, often without our attention or assistance.

> Can you see a tree grow?
> Can you watch the moon move?
> Can you witness a flower bloom?
> Can you perceive the changing of the tides?
> Can you observe a child grow up?

These things are noticeable only when observed *over time*. At any given moment, nothing seems to be happening to the tree or the moon or the flower or the tides or the child: yet their progress is unstoppable. Growth and change happen even when we don't see or notice them.

If you feel stuck in a season of waiting, that doesn't mean time is being wasted. Not from God's perspective, anyway. He's

The problem is that we
tend to focus only on
what we can see—and
what we can see barely
scratches the surface of
what is actually happening.

a zero-waste God. He is intentional, strategic, and exceptionally skilled at the whole sovereignty thing. He's going to hold up his end of the deal. *You* might be waiting, but *God* is always working, and he will bring his purposes to pass.

Our years of infertility were a season of waiting, but something was also happening all along: God was strengthening us. Building our faith. Drawing us closer to him. We learned not just to wait passively, but to wait actively—to expect that God was up to something on our behalf. This is the same principle the prophet Isaiah described when he wrote:

> But those who wait on the Lord
> Shall renew their strength;
> They shall mount up with wings like eagles,
> They shall run and not be weary,
> They shall walk and not faint. (Isaiah 40:31 NKJV)

Waiting on the Lord is never a waste. It only makes you stronger.

I can't tell you what waiting should look like for you, although the principles that follow include a few suggestions to get you started. But I know in my own life, waiting rarely means inaction. It's not a passive, bored, lazy, let-God-take-care-of-it-while-I-stare-at-the-wall approach to life. Instead, it means being faithful with what I know to do until God shows me otherwise.

What does that look like? Every person and circumstance is different, but here are a few possibilities.

- School: finish strong.
- Work: be honest and faithful.
- School or credit card debt: pay it down.
- Friends: be kind, faithful, present.
- Parents: show honor and love.
- Character: work on growing in areas the Holy Spirit has pointed out.

- Dating: try, try again, if that's something you want to do, and always treat people with respect, dignity, and purity.
- Spiritual growth: stay close to God and continue to grow.

You could probably add to that list. They are all goals you already have, I'm sure, it's just a matter of being faithful in the small things. Don't underestimate the power of perseverance, of just showing up, while you wait for things to become clearer.

Also, don't look down on the foundation you're laying with your small and consistent acts of obedience. When Israel began rebuilding the Jerusalem temple after a foreign army had destroyed it, some people mocked the new construction because it didn't measure up to their memories or expectations. God sent the prophet Zechariah to declare these words to the leaders: "Do not despise these small beginnings" (Zechariah 4:10). He said God himself rejoiced to see the work that had begun.

How often do we despise something God is rejoicing over because it's not moving fast enough, or it's not big enough, or it's not impressive enough in our limited perspective? If we could only see it from God's perspective, we would be overflowing with joy and expectation.

Don't resent the waiting. Instead, trust that God is working while you wait and that in him, nothing ever goes to waste. Often the most significant, beautiful changes are the ones that move the slowest and take the longest. Someday, you'll look back on this season and realize that God was playing the long game. He was doing a deep work that only became visible over time.

THE GRASS IS GREENER WHERE YOU WATER IT

The second principle for navigating the changing seasons of life is this:

> *The grass isn't greener on the other side—it's greener where you water it.*

That sounds like something you'd see on Pinterest, and I don't even know where I heard it, but it's true. We can spend so much time and mental energy wishing we had the neighbor's yard, metaphorically speaking, instead of pulling out the hose and giving our own yard some TLC. Ironically, the neighbor is probably looking at someone else's yard and wishing the same thing. Humans aren't very good at contentment.

I can't tell you how many singles I've talked to who would love nothing more than to get married. It's all they talk about. "Oh, my goodness, I just want to get married. You married people are so lucky. I can't wait. I'm so ready. I'm so lonely. I'm so thirsty."

But when I talk to people who are married, they'll often say things like, "Wow, I didn't know how good I had it when I was single. Marriage is challenging. Parenting is crazy. Single people need to value what they have."

Don't be that guy. Don't be that girl. Instead of wishing for what someone else has, invest in what is already yours. Lean into your season, grow where you're planted, flourish where you're found. You can't change the past or predict the future, so you might as well build a present you enjoy.

This requires work and commitment on your part. Remember, waiting doesn't look like inaction, but rather like faithfulness.

Why? Because being faithful is an investment in your future. It's watering what you have because you know it will grow into something good.

Yes, responding to the seasons of life might involve making some dramatic changes, so don't be afraid to take risks when the time is right. But it often means waiting patiently, being faithful day in and day out, even when life is not glamorous and no one notices your hard work. Patience can be the most difficult response of all, but your patience proves your faith. It shows that you understand growth comes from God.

If you're familiar with some of the stories in the Bible, you can probably think of a few examples of people who flourished where they were at, even when it was a less-than-ideal situation. Remember Joseph? He was sold into slavery as a teenager, but over time, he rose to the top of his master's household. Then he was thrown into prison for years, but eventually he rose to the top of the prison system. Then one day, literally overnight, he rose to the top of the Egyptian government when Pharaoh made him his right-hand administrator. Joseph couldn't be kept down because he maintained his integrity and work ethic no matter what happened. He flourished wherever he found himself, even when that included slavery or prison.

Remember Esther? She was an orphaned Israelite girl raised by her cousin, but through a crazy series of events, she became the queen of Persia. She must have felt out of control of her destiny many times along the way. She was a victim of a foreign empire that couldn't care less about her rights as a Jew, much less as a woman. Yet, God had a plan for her. As queen, she was ultimately able to save all of Israel from genocide.

Remember the apostle Paul? He started out persecuting Christians, but he responded radically to God's call and became a preacher and church planter. Everywhere he went, no matter what happened, he continued to serve God and people. The letters he wrote throughout his ministry comprise a large portion of the New Testament. Several of them were written from prison. Can you imagine how those months and years must have felt to him at the time? He must have thought he was wasting his life in jail when he could have had a much greater impact traveling and preaching and serving God. Yet, for the last two thousand years, those letters have continued to build the church. As it turned out, Paul had far greater influence from prison than he could have had traveling.

Water your own lawn. Make the grass around you as green as you can. Tomorrow, you might be somewhere else, or you might still be where you are today. You don't know. You can't know. So you might as well make the most of what you have. That's all God asks of you.

FIND YOUR LIGHT AND SHINE WHERE YOU ARE

Tyra Banks is an iconic actress, model, businesswoman, and television personality who hosted the reality show *America's Next Top Model* for twenty-four seasons. As she mentored up-and-coming models, she repeated a couple of phrases so often that they became synonymous with her method. One was "smize," which means smiling with your eyes; and another was "find your light," which means making sure your face is angled to get the best light for the camera, no matter how awkward or odd the modeling pose was.

Smizing is helpful when the lower half of your face is hidden behind a facemask, as the recent pandemic has shown. But I want to talk about the second phrase. *Find your light* is not just good advice when you're in front of a camera—it's good advice for life. The third principle for navigating change is this:

Find your light and shine where you are.

No matter how strange, unexpected, or uncomfortable your circumstances might be, there is always a way to shine. To work with what you have instead of complaining about it. To take advantage of what you are going through, not just survive it.

Deciding to find your light is a reflection of your attitude more than anything. Legendary author and pastor Charles Swindoll put it this way:

> The longer I live, the more I realize the impact of attitude on life. Attitude, to me, is more important than facts. It is more important than the past, than education, than money, than circumstances, than failure, than successes, than what other people think or say or do. It is more important than appearance, giftedness, or skill. It will make or break a company... a church... a home. The remarkable thing is we have a choice every day regarding the attitude we will embrace for that day.... I am convinced that life is 10 percent what happens to me and 90 percent of how I react to it.[11]

I especially love that last sentence. Much of life is out of your control, but that doesn't mean you are a victim of fate. Your response matters more than anything. You don't get to choose the hand you're dealt, but you do get to choose how you play it. If you react with faith, gratitude, positivity, generosity, creativity, integrity, and a strong work ethic, you can shine in any circumstance.

Remember, it's *your* light, not somebody else's. The angles are yours to discover. The camera is yours to dazzle. No one else has the unique opportunities you do, and no one else brings to the table what you have to offer.

HONOR AND ENJOY THE SEASON YOU ARE IN RIGHT NOW

The fourth and final principle to keep in mind when seasons come and go is this:

Honor and enjoy the season you are in right now.

Honoring something means you recognize its value and enjoying something means you recognize its contribution to your life. That doesn't mean you should lie to yourself about what you are going through or feeling. Be honest about the difficulties and disappointments, but also acknowledge the good things along the way.

Your life is already happening, as I said before. This is it. You're here, even if that feels a bit underwhelming at times. Don't wait for something or someone to bring you fulfillment or joy. If you can't be content now, you'll likely never be content, because joy, happiness, and contentment are choices you make even when the circumstances around you aren't exactly awesome.

Life is less about a destination and more about the journey, anyway. Too often, people attach their happiness or their satisfaction to a future accomplishment, a future spouse, a future family. Don't do that. Learn to celebrate *what* you have, *where* you are, and *who* you are today. Decide to honor and enjoy every stage of the journey.

I'm not advocating complacency or martyrdom, of course. Contentment is not the same thing as being lazy or giving up. You should always dream for more, and you should always work to achieve those dreams. Just dream and work from a satisfied place, not an empty place. From confidence, not insecurity. From a heart of gratitude, not a heart of bitterness.

***

Everything is beautiful in its own time and its own way, as Solomon reminded us, and there is a season for everything. Learn to see the beauty where you are. To value the season you are in rather than longing only for the future. Whether you are adding something new to your life, cutting out something old, or a little bit of both, embrace the place you're in.

Trust me, God is not as frustrated or impatient as you might be at times. He's excited about your life. He's proud of what you've accomplished and full of faith for what lies ahead. Let his perspective shift your attitude toward whatever season you are going through.

You've got a glorious, chaotic, beautiful, twisting, messy, rich life ahead of you, and God is with you every step of the way.

God is with you.

ANN'S STORY

"God, while there is immense pain, grief, and loss, and while I navigate uncharted waters, I want joy. I want peace. I'm not going to live another day like I lived this last year, focused on the loss and the darkness, in a victim-like state. Teach me to live with joy and peace and contentment—in a warrior-like state—while there is pain and heartache."

This was on January 1, 2018, a little over a year after my husband at the time had a traumatic brain injury, leaving us and our marriage in a dark, unexpected place.

That prayer changed my life. In that moment by myself on New Year's Day, I felt God take the weight and replace it with strength. Seasons of pain aren't foreign to me or to any of us. But seasons of pain that are grounded by joy and a deep peace were foreign. I was determined to have God change this in me—and he did.

For the next three years, I would go on a journey with God to create new, healthy habits—stretching my faith, my creativity, my mental and physical strength. Reckless hope and bold prayers became my normal. This season will not be wasted. It will be a sacred season.

I began waking up at 5:00 a.m. and spending my first 45-60 minutes alone with God every day in prayer. My circle got both wider and deeper. I committed to being intentional with my community. From my VOUS crew to my friends who are far from Jesus, I received love and loved well, consistently, with authenticity. Orange Theory became my new best (physical) friend, four to five days a week. I started an interior design business. Serving at church continued, but I leaned in even more, with more creativity and more energy. I started seeing my therapist again on a regular basis. With God, I created an ecosystem of healthy, faith-filled habits that produced joy even when pain was present.

Little did I know what God was preparing me for. That three-year season of not wasting a moment, forming new habits, and learning to live with pain and joy was for a purpose because, in 2020, my marriage ended unexpectedly and unwantedly. It was another traumatic moment in my life, but this time, I had three years of a new foundation built with God. Brick by brick.

Yes, the pain of the divorce was intense—the most intense pain I've faced in my forty-one years on this earth. There was suffering. There was (and still is) massive grief.

But those habits carried me through the trauma. Dare I say they allowed me to still experience both joy and peace? I dare. I didn't form those habits for the good times of life; they were for the hard times. I prayed for a change, walking hand-in-hand with Jesus, and he held my heart through it all. And now that I am on the other side, I'm still practicing my habits. There is no question that my best days are ahead of me. I'm better because of the last four and a half years.

I won't ever waste a season. I'm committed to watering my own lawn. To not only finding my light but shining it onto others. As I embark on a new season of being a single mom at the ripe age of forty-one, you better believe I'm honoring this season and that my habits are in full effect, every day, still. Thank you, Jesus!

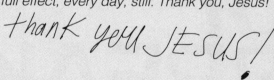

thank you JESUS!

07 BREAK UP OR BREAK DOWN

HAVE YOU EVER BEEN IN THE MIDDLE of watching a series on Netflix when one of your favorite characters was suddenly killed off? This person seemed to be essential, powerful, and destined for greatness in the plotline—and then the writers randomly wrote them out of the show. The sheer heartlessness of it all leaves you questioning the meaning of life.

But if you keep watching, you realize something. The tragedies and losses move the story forward. Characters and plotlines shift. People come and go. Storylines cross, separate, and cross again.

It's the way stories work, and it's the way life works.

When it comes to your life, though, you (and God, of course) are in charge of the storyline. You must do the cutting out, the killing off, the breaking up. You have to write the script of your life, not sit on the couch eating popcorn and watching in shock as your favorite character is shot or trampled or abducted by aliens or turned into a zombie. In other words, sometimes you have to make some hard choices about what you keep and what you get rid of in your life.

Right now, today, you might need to kill off something that you once considered irreplaceable. I'm not talking literal homicide—don't do that. But you should definitely consider, on a regular basis, whether or not you need to write a few things (or a person or two) out of the story of your life because they are not taking you where you need to go.

That is not easy. It takes courage. It takes wisdom. It takes foresight and perspective. You have to leave behind whatever is holding you back or your story will begin to drag, falter, and eventually fizzle out.

You have to be careful with this concept, especially if your personality lends itself to a hack-and-slash approach toward life, love, and work. You don't want to kill off parts of your life that should be valued and nurtured. And you definitely shouldn't view people as if their value depends solely on what they can offer you. That's selfish and toxic.

I'm sure you know the importance of being generous, patient, and faithful. But it's also possible to be generous to a fault. Patient to a fault. Loyal to a fault. That's a common problem, especially among good people who are trying to live good lives.

Why? Well, I'm not a psychologist, and I don't know you personally, of course. But I've had a lot of conversations with a lot of people, and a few themes stand out.

If you struggle with cutting things out of your life, it could be because *you are an incredibly loyal, altruistic, empathetic person.* That's a good thing, although it can be abused. Don't swing the pendulum the other way in self-defense just because you've been used and abused, though. Instead, learn how to care for yourself in a healthy, mature, God-focused, and others-focused way. We'll talk about that later on.

Maybe, though, you hold onto things that hold you back because *you can't imagine life without them.* It's not so much loyalty as it is dependency. You always saw that person, that career, that city, that title, that applause as an essential element in your existence.

Or maybe you hold onto things not because you think they are so amazing, but because *you are afraid the alternative will be even worse.* So you tolerate habits, people, activities, and choices that you know are not doing you any good out of fear of change.

Again, I'm not trying to psychoanalyze you here. I'm also not saying you have some pathological, fatal attraction to toxic things. But you are human, and as a fellow human, I get it. I do it, too. I often hold on to things that are breaking me down instead of breaking up with them and moving on.

Maybe you're familiar with Marie Kondo, the Japanese organizing consultant whose books have sold millions of copies. Her trademarked "KonMarie Method" for tidying up your house focuses on keeping only the things that "speak to the heart," and discarding things that "no longer spark joy." She says you should thank those items for their contribution to your life and then let them go.[12]

That's good advice for more than just your house. Maybe you need to Marie Kondo your mental space. Or Marie Kondo your time management. Or Marie Kondo your relationships. What still speaks to you? You should probably keep it. What no longer sparks joy? Maybe it's time to thank it, honor it—and then let it go.

BREAKING UP IS HARD

Knowing when to let go is a life skill that you'll use across every sphere of life, from dreams to jobs to relationships. It's especially important, though, when it comes to romantic relationships. While much of this book has been about singleness in general, I want to spend a few minutes looking specifically at dating and love—and at some things you need to break up with before they break you down.

Breakups are a time-honored part of being single, after all. Unless you live in a culture where marriages are arranged, breakups are one of the occupational hazards of dating. Odds are, you've already had a breakup or two. Maybe it was your sixth-grade crush. Maybe it was your high school sweetheart. Maybe it was someone you'd dated for years and you were sure marriage was in your future, but it didn't work out that way. You broke up, and it was probably—at least a little bit—painful and messy.

If you're still hurting from a recent breakup, hang on. We'll talk more about dealing with heartbreak in the next chapter. First, though, we need to acknowledge that breakups can be a good thing.

Have you ever stayed too long in a bad relationship? Things started out great, but as time went on, you started seeing the manipulation, the character flaws, the different values, the immaturity, the abuse, the addiction, the narcissism. Eventually,

Side note: if you are married, I'm not encouraging you to break up with your spouse. Quite the opposite. Fight for that relationship.

you

fight for

you realized that not only were you not *good* together, you were *bad* together. Staying in that romantic relationship was causing real damage.

So one or both of you made the bold, painful decision to break up. Afterward, you probably felt a mix of emotions: grief, regret, guilt, anger, but also relief. Because even though you were going to have to walk through some difficult days, you knew things were finally back on track.

Breaking up is hard to do, to quote another classic oldie. But it's not as hard as trying to force something to work that is headed toward self-destruction sooner or later. Despite the pain, breaking up with someone who is wrong for you is the best thing you can do. It's an act of love and wisdom.

DawnCheré broke up with me multiple times while we were dating. We're married now, so she obviously realized the error of her ways. The first time she broke up with me was the day before Thanksgiving. (Who does that?) It was heartless and cruel. It ruined my Thanksgiving. I haven't been able to eat mashed potatoes since.

Hard as it was, I respected her more for it. She was honest with her journey and her heart. Marriage isn't something to rush into, and I had to trust her hesitation and her decisions. I had no hesitation at all, which means that either I was far more spiritual than her, or I knew I was getting the better end of the deal. I'd vote for the latter.

Should you break up? That's your choice to make. No one else knows the situation, the person you're dating, and you like you do. Don't be afraid to do it if it's necessary, but don't be too quick to do it either. Lean into love and let wisdom and the Holy Spirit guide you.

Side note: if you are married, I'm not encouraging you to break up with your spouse. Quite the opposite. Fight for that relationship. Get counseling, get away as a couple, get tools to help you communicate, get whatever you need to give your marriage every possible chance to flourish. Assuming there is no abuse or other clear grounds for separation, don't break up with each other, but *do* break up with wrong ways of communicating or resolving conflicts, with unforgiveness, or anything else that is coming between you.

That brings me to the main point: often, the real breakup needs to be with *wrong mindsets*, not with people. You can be with the right person but have the wrong idea about relationships. If you don't correct your misconceptions, those wrong ideas might sabotage or even destroy what should have been a good thing.

We're going to consider four mindsets that deserve to be dumped. Broken up with. Ghosted. Unfollowed. Deleted from your contacts. I've had so many conversations with single people in which I've either talked about these four points or wished I had. These are things that will get in your way and steal your joy, and if you don't break up with them, they'll break you down. It's time to break up with fairy tales, feelings, fate, and failure.

FAIRY TALES

The first thing you need to break up with is fairy tales. What is a fairy tale? It's a story you make up in your head that you wish were true. It's a fantasy, a dream, an impossibly perfect ending that is heavy on imagination and light on reality.

You should dream, of course. You should have a vision for the kind of marriage and family you want. Having clear dreams and vision will help keep your dating decisions aligned with your long-term values.

> What kind of relationship do you want to have?
> What things will you share?
> What will you accomplish together?
> What values will you have in common?

> How will you handle disagreement and conflict?
> How will you treat each other and talk to each other?
> What will your relationship look like in ten years, twenty years, fifty years?

The problem, though, is that if you don't have a realistic idea of what dating, love, marriage, and family look like, you might fall in love with a fairy tale rather than a person. You need a clear vision of what is actually possible, not what you wish were possible.

My parents are fantastic examples of love and commitment, so I know firsthand how their positive example gave me a realistic view of marriage; but unfortunately, they are the exception. While I hope you had a similar experience with your own parents, it's possible you didn't. Maybe your experience was far different, even dysfunctional. Maybe your parents divorced when you were young. Or maybe they were married, but they were miserable. Maybe in your home, physical abuse was part of your narrative. Or maybe family members weren't physically violent, but they were verbally abusive. Maybe when people in your home were stressed out, they self-medicated, and you grew up around addiction and substance abuse. Maybe your parents had a toxic, codependent relationship. Maybe you grew up with neglect, abandonment, or loneliness.

If any of that describes your story, I'm so sorry. You deserved better then, and you deserve better now. It's hard to find "better," though, if you don't know what you're looking for. And that's my point.

We learn from what we watch. That's how humans work. We might not remember learning it, but most of what you and I know about relationships, family, and social interactions is learned behavior. We are deeply influenced by the people who surround us, whether or not we realize it.

At some point, though, we become self-aware enough to realize that we don't want the dysfunction we witnessed as a child or young person. We don't know what we want, but we know what we don't want.

"I'll tell you one thing, I don't want to be my dad."

"All I know is I'm not going to be like my mom."

"My family was so dysfunctional. I don't want that."

"I'm not going to do that to my kids, I promise you."

This is where the problem starts, though. We can't create something we've never seen before, so we start searching for a reference. We look for a positive mental picture of what a good relationship is.

And what do we find?

Fairy tales.

Happily-ever-after stories that gloss over the complexities and nuances of human love and family life.

I have nothing against fairy tales, but I certainly don't believe we should build our future on them. That's why they're called fairy tales. They are not real. They're not meant to be role models. And if you base your vision for the future on a fantasy you've made up, you're going to end up hurt, disillusioned, or both.

The first fairy tale premise you have to break up with is that all you have to do is find "the one," and you'll live happily ever after.

That's a myth. Not the part about a happy future, because you can have a thrilling and fulfilling life as a married couple. I'm a decade and a half into this, and it only gets better.

The myth is that getting married is the finish line. That once you've found your true love, worked out your differences, defeated your dragons, and made it to the altar, the rest is just an epilogue.

That doesn't just sound impossible, it sounds boring. The truth is that getting married is truly just the beginning. You only live happily ever after if you're willing to put in the work every day.

The day after the wedding.
The day after the honeymoon.
The day after that big fight.
The day after your baby is born.
The day after you are fired from your job.
The day after you buy a house.

The day after your career starts to take off.
The day after the difficult diagnosis.
The day after you retire.

Happiness comes with learning and growing, loving and forgiving, sticking out the tough times and laughing through the fun ones. Happily ever after is not a destination. It's a journey. Fairy tales tell you that happiness awaits at the finish line, but a healthy relationship based on a realistic vision understands that happiness is found where you look for it.

The second fairy tale premise to break up with is that *someone has to be rescued.* Don't wait to be rescued, and don't look for someone who needs to be rescued. Marriage is about two people walking together, not one person constantly saving the other and then dragging them along like Shrek and Princess Fiona. Speaking of Shrek, that might be the most realistic tale of them all (which isn't saying much) because it shows the dysfunction every relationship experiences.

If you're investing in the stock market, you look at potential. If you're investing in a business start-up, you look at potential. But when you're choosing a spouse, don't focus on potential—focus on *patterns*. Marry someone based on who they are now and the track record they have to date, not on who they might become if you're lucky.

You can't guarantee your beloved will change. You aren't Jesus. You're not called to save your partner, heal your partner, sanctify your partner, or perfect your partner. You're called to walk with them, to love them, to believe in them, to cheer for them. Fall in love with the person in front of you, not with some future version of them you hope will materialize.

"But you don't know him!" you protest. "I know the real him. I know his heart. He's trying so hard. He has good intentions. He just needs someone to believe in him."

Yo! He's cheated on you three times! You have a fairy tale vision of a relationship.

"You don't understand," you say. "When I'm alone with her,

she's different. I know the real her! She loves me. She's good for me. She's the one for me."

But bro, she's verbally abusing you, she's controlling you—and everyone around can see it. You're losing yourself. You're losing your confidence. You're compromising who you are. She's not good for you, and she is not right for you.

You aren't your partner's knight in shining armor, nor are you a sleeping princess in need of a magic kiss. You're both human beings with strength, courage, dignity, a calling, and the Holy Spirit. Of course you'll lean on each other a lot, but as a general rule, you should be walking in the same direction with the same passion, using your gifts and callings to complement each other—not continually rescuing each other.

The third fairy tale premise you need to leave behind is that *the best (or only) kind of love is love at first sight.* Fairy tales sell us a passionate, all-consuming, never-look-back kind of love that magically changes everything in an instant. "I saw her, and I fell in love!" "He's my Prince Charming." "She's my Sleeping Beauty."

Maybe that's your story, but it's risky stuff. Not because love can't happen instantaneously, but because love has to go deeper than what you can see, and it has to last longer than a flash of passion.

You fell in love with that person at first sight? Okay. But do you think you might need to have a few real conversations now? You don't know what they believe. You haven't seen how they behave under pressure. You have no idea what their credit score is.

Love at first sight is wonderful—as long as spending time together and engaging in heartfelt conversation brings depth and solidity to the relationship. But don't put your trust in the goosebumps you felt when he slid into your DMs. In the way your heart pounded when she matched with you on Tinder. In the spark that happened when your eyes met across the room.

I'm not knocking those things, because they are beautiful.

just maybe

Maybe that's your story, but it's risky stuff.

They are awesome, and you'll remember them the rest of your life. But keep them in their place. They might be the beginning of love, but they're not the fullness of love.

You shouldn't have to force love or rush love. Solomon wrote, "Do not arouse or awaken love until it so desires" (Song of Solomon 8:4). In other words, let love grow naturally. Let it take its time. Allow it to go through the natural stages of growth and plateaus that long-term relationships must experience.

The love-at-first-sight myth doesn't just make people jump into love too quickly—it can also keep them from finding love at all. Some people wouldn't recognize love if it hit them over the head with a box of chocolates. They are convinced they need to feel something magical and irresistible right away, and unless that happens, they won't allow themselves to love.

But love doesn't always start that way. It *often* doesn't start that way. A lot of times, it takes three steps forward and two back. Just ask DawnCheré about all those breakups.

I avoid being a matchmaker for obvious reasons, but there have been a few occasions when my wife or I have offered to introduce single people we know to someone we think might be a possibility. We aren't trying to play Cupid, and we're not asking anyone to go out and buy a ring. We just hope they'll give the other person a chance. But often, based solely on a photo—a static, two-dimensional, freaking profile pic—they won't even take the person out for coffee.

I understand that attraction matters. Yes, you need to like

them physically. But have you ever considered that "not your type" might *be* your type if you just gave that person a chance? That attraction could begin through conversation? That hearts take time to connect, and walls require patience to come down, and bodies were designed to respond to intimacy, rather than being the initiators of intimacy? We're all fighting gravity anyway, so your top criteria better not be physical appearance. Prince Charming isn't going to look like Prince Charming forever.

Some girls are looking for tall, dark, and handsome. You need to break up with that idea and instead look for trustworthy, hardworking, and honest. Some guys are looking for sexy, beautiful, and fit. Break up with that criteria and look for smart, bold, and confident. Again, I understand that physicality matters—but "love at first sight" too easily morphs into "lust based on what I'm looking at," and that's superficial and misleading, not to mention selfish.

While we're on the subject of superficial attraction, take note that porn is a fairy tale. I'm not here to judge you, and I'm not going to tell you what constitutes porn, nor what you should watch. Remember, though, that porn is intentionally crafted to feed into fantasies. It's fake. It's a myth. It will not give you an accurate picture of anything: of love, of sex, of the female body, of the male body, of relationships, of happiness. If you fill your mind with fairy tales, if you condition your hormones to respond to fantasies, how do you expect to have a healthy relationship with a real human?

These three myths—that marriage automatically leads to happily ever after, that someone always has to be rescued, and that love happens at first sight—are some of the most common fairy tales, but you can probably think of others.

The point is this: don't live in a fantasy world, and don't attach your happiness to what is not real. Break up with fairy tales, or they'll break you down.

FEELINGS

Feelings →

The second thing you need to break up with when it comes to relationships is your feelings. I'm not saying feelings don't matter, of course. God created love, passion, and desire, and they are fantastic. I'm a huge fan. The problem, though, is that our culture is in love with the *idea* of love, and it often makes feelings the final arbiter of our decisions.

> "Listen to your heart."
> "Do what you want."
> "Do what makes you happy."
> "Follow your feelings."
> "The heart knows what it wants."

One of the greatest obstacles to relationships is having the wrong definition of love. I meet smart, educated, successful people who still reduce love to emotions. If love is nothing more than feelings, then it will come and go on a whim. Limiting your view of love to feelings and hormones sells it short. Love is so much more beautiful, complex and nuanced than that. Here's what the apostle Paul wrote about love:

> Love is patient, love is kind.
> It does not envy, it does not boast, it is not proud.
> It does not dishonor others, it is not self-seeking, it is not easily angered, it keeps no record of wrongs.
> Love does not delight in evil but rejoices with the truth.
> It always protects, always trusts, always hopes, always perseveres. Love never fails. (1 Corinthians 13:4-8)

This definition is fascinating to me because none of the things that follow the word love are emotions. They are decisions. They are actions. They are character traits. Why? Because love is far more than a feeling. As the great author and thinker C. S. Lewis wrote, "Love, in the Christian sense, does not mean emotion. It is a state not of the feelings but of the will; that state of the will which we have naturally about ourselves, and must learn to have about other people."[13]

I've noticed that the things I genuinely want are often at odds with my feelings. I want to focus on my walk with God, but my feelings sometimes disagree. I want to focus on my family, but my feelings sometimes disagree. I want to be more patient with people, but my feelings usually disagree. I want to eat right this year, but my feelings *always* disagree.

The good news is, we don't have to follow our feelings. We can make our own decisions. As followers of Jesus, we are filled with the Holy Spirit. The power and wisdom of God are within us to make wise choices and live disciplined lives.

When we make positive decisions, positive feelings will eventually follow.

FATE

The third thing you need to break up with is a reliance on fate. Fate is the idea that you're not in control, that somehow an impersonal force is deciding significant parts of your life. It's expressed in phrases such as, "Everything happens for a reason," "As fate would have it," "I'm leaving it up to the universe," and so on.

Blaming fate is often a way of avoiding responsibility for our actions or inactions. It sounds poetic and romantic and humble

As Christians, sometimes we substitute God for fate. That is, we absolve ourselves of responsibility by invoking "God's will" or "divine providence."

to entrust our future to destiny, but fate isn't a thing. It's not real. Fate doesn't think or act. It doesn't know you or care about you. It's a vague concept that is synonymous with luck and chance. We give fate way too much credit.

As Christians, sometimes we substitute God for fate. That is, we absolve ourselves of responsibility by invoking "God's will" or "divine providence." Let me be clear: I believe in God's providence and sovereignty. He's in control. He reigns in the universe. He's not shocked or surprised by what happens to us. He actively guides the steps of those who follow him.

But you still have to be responsible for your actions. When it comes to relationships, you can't just expect fate or God to do for you what you can legitimately do for yourself. Don't blame your love life, or lack thereof, on God if you never do anything to improve it.

- Take the initiative. Take risks.
- Be vulnerable and let your heart feel again.
- Be wise and loving toward others.
- Keep your eyes open.
- Seek healing from past trauma.
- Pray. Then flirt. Then pray some more.
- Work on your character and personality quirks.
- Don't be weird. But don't be too ordinary, either.
- Live responsibly, building a life for the future.
- Be holy and pure, honoring your future spouse today.
- Save money, pay off debts, build your career. Kids are expensive. Trust me on this one.
- Invest in many relationships. You never know when a friend might become more than a friend.
- Get outside yourself, live beyond yourself, become generous.
- And please, for the love of God, ask someone out on a date.

Fate cannot override your choices. God can, of course, but he's the one who created free will in the first place, and it's almost scary how much power and freedom he has given each of us. Yes, you face all the usual human limitations, but you also have a great deal of say in your life. That's my point here.

Trusting fate leads us to believe in myths. Some of these myths are beautiful, though. We want to believe them. We tell them to ourselves when we feel lonely. "There's only one person in the universe for me. I'm looking for my soulmate, for that one person. We are destined to be together."

That sounds beautiful. I love that, but it's full of loopholes. Play that idea out in your head. Take it to its logical extreme.

What would happen if, while I'm married to DawnCheré, I were to say, "Oh shoot. We made a mistake. We chose wrong. We were close, but we weren't the one person in the universe for each other." Would I end our great marriage on the off chance the universe has some greater, undiscovered bliss waiting for me? Would she leave me because someone else is her soulmate, and I should have been friend-zoned from the beginning? I hope you can see how pointless that line of thought is.

It gets worse. If we were wrong for each other, we would have started a chain reaction of wrong choices. The people we were supposed to marry would then marry other people who are also wrong for them, and the people those people should marry will be left to choose wrong life partners, and so on, and so forth, forever. Imagine the number of marriages that would be ruined. The number of children brought into the world who should never have existed. This would go from a one-person problem to a seven-billion-person problem all because we said, "I do" instead of "I don't."

Ridiculous, right? So is blaming your love life on fate. Fate is not a matchmaker. People from Western cultures often critique cultures in which marriages are arranged—and then want fate to arrange their own marriage. Think about that. I'm not advocating we let parents choose our life partners, but they'd probably do a better job than fate. At least parents are real.

DawnCheré and I made a grown-up decision to get married. That was our choice as consenting, semi-mature adults. We made a covenant, a promise. There is immense beauty in that because it respects our choices and our dignity. We are the right people for each other because *we decided we were.*

When we were dating, of course there were butterflies, and romance, and starry-eyed dreams, and sweaty palms, and beating hearts. We have hundreds of memories of falling in love. But *falling* in love is also about *learning* to love. About *investing* in love. About nurturing a growing romance and letting our hearts become one. Because along with the butterflies, there were some bats. Along with the starry-eyed dreams, there were some misunderstandings. Along with the sweaty palms and beating hearts, there were some mean words, hurt feelings and humble apologies.

That's normal. It didn't mean fate didn't want us together. It meant we were two young people who had a lot to learn about love and each other. We never handed over the keys of our hearts to fate, though. We kept our eyes open and made our own choices, and we continue to stand by those choices.

Please don't think that I'm blaming you if you're single. First, because blame is not even a good way to look at it, since singleness is not a problem, sin, disappointment, or even a negative. Second, because there are a lot of things beyond your control in this messy world. Third, because love and marriage take two people, and you can't control anyone else, nor should you try. Those three disclaimers are important. But none of them cuts you totally out of the picture. They just ground you in reality.

Believing in fate, though, *ignores* reality. It creates excuses: "God chose this for me. The relationship wasn't his will. I guess I was meant to be single. Marriage and family just weren't in the cards for me. This is my lot in life, my cross to bear."

I've heard people say, "I'll meet someone in church." Or,

"God is going to bring me a spouse." It sounds so beautiful and holy. "God is going to give me the person of my dreams."

I want to say, "Yes, but do you have any part to play in that process? Do you need to go outside for this to happen?"

"No, he can bring the man of my dreams to my house."

I hope you are attracted to FedEx guys, then, because that's all you've got to work with here.

The wisdom of Scripture is, "He who finds a wife finds what is good" (Proverbs 18:22). The last time I checked, the word "find" is a verb. There's an action involved. You've got to do something.

"God is going to bring me the wife I want, so I'll stand over here with my homeys, scan the room once in a while, and put the vibe out. Let God work a miracle, you know?"

No, I don't know. And it won't work. She's not going to miraculously float into your arms. You're going to have to walk over and talk to her. Start with, "Hi!" Then be normal. Be respectful. Just talk. That might be the real miracle.

Remember, there's a fine line between searching and stalking. Guys, especially, don't be creepy. Quit staring at the girl throughout the entire worship service. It's weird. Don't be weird.

Also, don't be too cool. Or too dramatic. Or too bored. Or too self-centered.

Don't be too spiritual, either. "Last night, I was in my prayer closet, and the Lord led me to you." She's going to run, and I can't blame her.

Don't be shady, either. If you're crushing on someone, don't slide into their DMs late at night, saying, "I saw you at church yesterday." If that's the case, why didn't you walk over and start a conversation yesterday?

Yes, she might ignore you. She might turn down your invitation to coffee. That hurts. But at least you did what you could, and your courage counts for more than you might realize.

Some girls say, "I'm dating Jesus." Cool. But if you're dating Jesus and you're complaining about it, what guy on earth stands a chance? There's nowhere to go from there! Have high expectations, but don't make this impossible on yourself. Faithfulness and a growth mindset should be non-negotiables in a boyfriend, but walking on water is an extra.

If a guy is brave enough to talk to you, cut him a little slack. The fact he's showing interest in you doesn't necessarily mean he's desperate or thirsty. Ideally, it means he sees your value and that he is attracted to you because you are amazing, spiritual, and intelligent, not just beautiful. Until he proves otherwise, give him the benefit of the doubt. That doesn't mean you have to go out with him if you're genuinely not interested, but don't write him off just because shutting down a conversation feels safer than opening your heart.

Faith is not a cop-out. Belief in God is not an excuse for fear. Trust is not justification for disengaging with scary life choices. I hear a lot of people saying, "God chose this for me." While I don't pretend to know the mind of God for your life, if you're not careful, you'll blame God or fate for the dumb stuff you do or the opportunities you miss because you didn't take the first step.

You are called to live by faith, but faith without works is dead (James 2:17). Fate leads us to apathy, but faith leads us to action. Faith turns us into responsible human beings who trust God enough to take tangible steps toward a positive future.

I don't know if you will get married or if you even want to get married. Just don't allow yourself to become apathetic or irresponsible, blaming God and fate, complaining about a situation that is within your power to change. Break up with fate and embrace faith.

FAILURE

The fourth and final thing we need to break up with is failure. Specifically, I'm talking about failure caused by relationships that didn't turn out how they could or should have.

Much—maybe most—of the pain in our lives comes from relationships. I don't mean to minimize other kinds of pain, but broken relationships have the power to hurt us so deeply we may think we'll never fully recover. Many of our deepest hurts, many of the hardest things for us to get over, are attached to people. And if we're not careful, one bad relationship can damage all of our other relationships

Maybe your relational pain was caused by *someone failing you.* Your dad cheated on your mom. Your mom was never there for you. A family member emotionally or physically abused you. A boyfriend promised you the world and then disappeared. Your husband vowed, "Until death do us part," but then he walked out and never came back.

The wound is deep and the pain is real. It is so present, so loud, that it holds you back from your future. It taints and poisons the potentially good relationships that come your way because you are afraid of getting hurt again.

The thing is—and I wish there were an easier way to say this—relationships are *always* going to require you to trust again, to believe again, to hope again, to risk again. That doesn't mean denying the pain of the past, but it does mean not allowing that pain to create more pain. You can acknowledge the trauma you've lived, find healing as much as possible, and continue forward with a healthy mindset. It takes work, though, and maybe some counseling or therapy, prayer, self-education, and time.

Maybe your relational pain was caused not by someone failing you, but by *you failing someone else.* Perhaps you were the one who hurt someone, who cheated, who abused another

You were not created to live under the constant weight of guilt and shame. That sense of failure will break you down. You can't carry it.

created

CREATED

YOU

person, who walked out. If that's true, acknowledge your failure, but don't let yourself be defined by it. Just because you made mistakes doesn't make you a mistake. Just because you failed doesn't mean you are a failure.

You were not created to live under the constant weight of guilt and shame. That sense of failure will break you down. You can't carry it. Only Jesus can, and he offers you the grace to move on from your mistakes. That doesn't change what happened, and it doesn't absolve you from consequences—you might need to make apologies or restitution. It doesn't erase the past, but it does release your future. You can't enjoy today or have hope for tomorrow if you're beating yourself up over a mistake from yesterday.

Maybe your relational pain was caused by *wrong or unhealthy sexual experiences.* The Bible says that sexual immorality is the only sin we commit against our own body (1 Corinthians 6:18). The intimacy, connection, and vulnerability that come with sex are beautiful, and they bind two hearts together. But when the context of that sexual encounter is toxic or harmful, they can work against us. Yes, your body and your life are yours to govern, but sexual intimacy with the wrong person or in the wrong context can have far-reaching consequences. In particular, it can damage your confidence and identity and bring you under a cloud of guilt that will only hold you back.

If you find yourself living with shame because of past sexual activity, you need to let that go. Jesus does not see you as dirty, or broken, or rejected, or shameful. He loves you, and your value has never changed in his eyes. What happened is in the past. It doesn't change who you are, what you're worth, or what you can expect in the future. Don't let a wrong view of purity or virginity destroy your confidence. Whether the failure you've experienced is due to someone else's actions, mistakes you made, sexual immorality, or anything else, you can't live there. You can't stay there and move forward with your life.

Keep in mind that breaking up with failure is not just about moving past a broken relationship or trauma in the past. Sometimes we internalize failure so much that it becomes a self-fulfilling prophecy. We see ourselves as failures, so we fail. We see ourselves as quitters, so we quit.

That's when failure becomes a cycle, but it's a cycle that can be broken. If we are going to break up with failure, we have to break up with breaking up itself. We have to stop stopping. We have to quit quitting.

Past failure does not guarantee future failure. If anything, it helps protect us because we can learn from our mistakes and walk with greater wisdom. We need to look at our failings through the lenses of grace, hope, and faith. They are part of our story, but they don't get to write our story.

Of course, no relationship is perfect. I wish I could say that if you just follow seven simple steps, all of your relationships will be perfect, easy, and free of pain—but it doesn't work that way. We let each other down. We offend each other. We snap at each other. We hold each other to standards that aren't fair.

This means you're going to have to deal with future failures, not just past ones. You have to go into any relationship understanding that two fallible human beings trying to love each other and do life together will make quite a few mistakes.

This doesn't justify relational failures or abuse—they are wrong, and they need to be addressed and changed. And I am certainly not condoning abuse or toxicity, especially when it's always one person doing the hurting and the other person doing the forgiving, or when the abuse is coming from a person with an imbalance of power. If you're experiencing this kind of abuse, it needs to stop. Don't stay in a relationship that is dangerous to your soul, your body, or your family. Make the necessary changes to protect your life and your dignity.

Even in a healthy, balanced relationship, though, people will make mistakes. Good intentions don't automatically make for good actions. We will always need grace and forgiveness. When mistakes happen, give each other space and time to grow. Hold people up when they are weak instead of tearing them down or walking out on them.

Rather than becoming accustomed to the endless cycle of loving, fighting, offending, and breaking up, only to start all over with another person, choose to break up with relational failure. Choose to break up with breaking up.

I'm not saying you should assume whoever you next fall in love with is "the one," but don't assume they *aren't* the one just because all your past romances have ended in heartbreak. You are not doomed to fail or destined to be hurt. Sure, you've had your share of pain, and you've probably made your share of mistakes. But those do not define you, and they don't determine your destiny.

So, whether others have failed you or you have failed others, or a little bit of both, today is a new day. No matter what has happened in the past, you can get back up and you can keep on going.

Break up with failure, before it breaks you down.

***

Whether you are breaking up with a relational myth or an actual person, breakups are a messy business all around. You might make mistakes along the way. You might suffer some heartbreak, as we'll see in the next chapter. Love is complicated and people are unpredictable, as you know all too well.

But remember, if you break up with the mindsets and misconceptions that sabotage love, if you break up with fairy tales and feelings and fate and failures, you'll be in a much stronger place. A much healthier place. Not just to meet your dream spouse, but to build a life together, and a family, and a future.

DANI'S STORY

The mistakes of my past do not define my future.

I was raised in a Christian home and went to a Wesleyan school from kindergarten to twelfth grade. My parents are active leaders in their church and have been married for over fifty years. Yes, I was a regular church kid. I had the best example and a world-class education. However, I learned about relationships the hard way.

I got married after law school, and life seemed perfect. I was living in D.C. in a fairy tale, but the butterflies disappeared, and life got real. I was frustrated, depressed, and disappointed. I didn't know how I had gotten to where I was. Not surprisingly, I made a lot of mistakes. I had wrong expectations and unhealthy views about women, relationships, and sex. I thought life should be like what I saw on TV or on a computer screen, which led to my divorce. I am at peace with that failure now, but it took a long time to give myself grace and forgive my past errors.

So, I moved to Miami and did what most recently divorced men do when they move to Miami in their mid-thirties: I went nuts. New city, new job, new car, new everything. I was determined to have a fresh start. But I didn't count on the guilt and shame of my past failures traveling with me.

I dated great women. I learned more about people in that period than ever before in my life. I saw the good and the bad. But something was missing. My faith was not well, and I was looking for refuge from the pain in all the wrong places.

Then I went to a midweek church service in a middle school in Wynwood, and everything changed. Over five years later, I see how I first needed to mend my vertical relationship with God to then have a healthy horizontal relationship with a woman. I also learned that I needed to heal from the trauma of my past in order to move into the future God intended for me to live.

It wasn't always pretty. Along the way, I've hurt people and made tough decisions. I've ended relationships and ceased seeing certain people. I didn't always know what I wanted, but I was definitely learning to identify what I didn't want. I realized that sometimes the best thing I could do for someone was to break up with them, because if you know it's wrong, it's unfair to the other person to continue.

God freed me of the guilt and shame. I understand that my mistakes never stopped God from loving me. He was preparing me for the next great chapter in my life, but I had to do the work, put action behind words, and live out my faith. I had to acknowledge my past, be truthful with myself, heal in the present, and look toward the future in faith and grace.

Fast forward, and God gave me the opportunity to turn lessons into actions. Six months ago, in an intimate backyard ceremony (during a pandemic), Pastor Rich officiated a beautiful wedding ceremony for my wife and me. Something he told us will now always be a part of our marriage values: "The grass is greener where you water it." I now know that love and relationships require work every day. Happiness is where we look for it, and it is attainable when we decide to put selfish desires aside in pursuit of enduring joy.

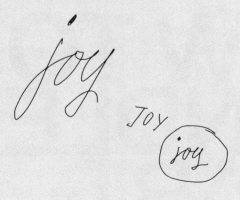

joy

JOY

joy

08 HOW TO HANDLE HEART-BREAK

I DON'T DO WELL WITH BLOOD. Especially my own. Who does, right? If you enjoy the sight of your own blood, there is obviously something wrong with you.

For me, it goes beyond an instinct for self-preservation. It's almost a phobia. I have a visceral reaction to blood, to shots, or really to anything that involves violence against my body. When I have blood drawn, I have to lie down and I want someone to hold my hand. When I get shots, I faint. Not exaggerating. I'm not proud of that, but I can't change it.

The birth of my kids was especially exciting. And by exciting, I mean terrifying. I couldn't let on, though, since I had to be strong for DawnCheré, which is a joke because she's the strongest person I know. All three of my kids were born via C-section, and I hid behind a curtain, not watching, just holding a camera up over the edge to video the birth for us to watch later. (Well, for DawnCheré to watch later.)

It's hard to hold a camera steady when you're struggling just to remain conscious. And yet, nobody wants to give me any credit for all my suffering and sacrifice during the birth. Weird.

Anyway, this issue with blood and shots is bad enough when it comes to my own life and family. But then there are the people who have recently broken a bone or had surgery and love to show off their scar or a picture of the wound. And they want to narrate in excruciating detail what happened and how bad it looked.

I finally have to say, "Bro, stop, I don't need to know all that. TMI. I'm sorry for your pain, but I'm nauseated just listening to you. And no, please don't show me the X-rays."

It's as if they want me to feel their pain. I can't help them, though, because I'm just trying to keep from losing my lunch as I listen to their descriptions of incisions, stitches, and bodily fluids. It's too much. I can't.

Wounds in the body are so visible, so painful, so traumatic that we can't help but talk about them. But what about wounds of the heart? They are not visible. You can't carry around a pho-

heartbreak. You can't measure your pain in stitches, as Shawn Mendes reminded us a few years back. And yet, this inner pain can affect your life more than any physical wound.

Just like twisted ankles, broken bones and vaccinations, heartbreak is a nearly inevitable element of human life. You can't love deeply without being vulnerable, and you can't allow flawed humans close to your heart without exposing your soul to some level of pain. To quote from the great C.S. Lewis once more:

> To love at all is to be vulnerable. Love anything, and your heart will certainly be wrung and possibly be broken. If you want to make sure of keeping it intact, you must give your heart to no one, not even to an animal. Wrap it carefully round with hobbies and little luxuries; avoid all entanglements; lock it up safe in the casket or coffin of your selfishness. But in that casket—safe, dark, motionless, airless—it will change. It will not be broken; it will become unbreakable, impenetrable, irredeemable.[14]

Love always has the potential for heartbreak. And yet, we must love. We were created to love. We long to love and be loved.

Which means we'd better be good at allowing ourselves to be healed of heartbreak.

HEARTS WERE MADE TO HEAL

Of all human relationships, the ones most vulnerable to heartache are the romantic ones. Just listen to Adele. Or Taylor Swift. Or pretty much any country singer.

If you've had your heart broken in love too many times and now you're gun shy, that is understandable. Heartbreak is an occupational hazard of romance, and it's simple logic. You want to marry the right person, but you can't find the right person until you've spent time with people who may or may not be the right person. That means opening up your heart to them. And if the relationship doesn't work out, a piece of your heart is at risk. It's the very definition of vulnerability.

People who date are incredibly brave. It takes courage to put yourself out there, especially if you've already been hurt a few times. If you're in this stage right now, then yes, you should guard your heart—but don't lock it away completely. Don't let the fear of pain rob you of the joys of intimacy.

> To be loved, you must love.
> To be known, you must be vulnerable.
> To receive, you must give.
> To be secure, you must trust.
> To be intimate, you must expose your heart.
> To find a soulmate, you must bare your soul.

Your heart can be hurt in any relationship, of course, not just romantic ones. And as we saw in the previous chapter, when you import pain and failure from past relationships into the present, it doesn't work out well for anyone. If you are carrying hurt and heartbreak from broken relationships with family, friends, colleagues, romantic interests, or exes, it's crucial to find as much healing and wholeness as you can.

Hearts were made to heal. It's not easy, it doesn't happen overnight, and there might be some things that don't ever fully go away. But if you turn to God, you can find divine healing and comfort from the heartbreak you've experienced. God does not faint at the sight of blood, and he doesn't shut you down when you talk to him about your trauma. His heart is drawn to hurt. His mercy and compassion are stirred by pain.

The psalmist wrote, "The Lord is close to the brokenhearted and saves those who are crushed in spirit" (Psalm 34:18). And, "He heals the brokenhearted and binds up their wounds"

God is that safe place for your heart. The healing might take time, but God is with you throughout the process, supporting you, sustaining you, protecting you, insulating you from further harm.

(Psalm 147:3). Even if God has felt far away, know that he is close to you. His healing hands are binding your wounds and completing the process of healing in your heart.

Think about what the word "bind" means. It has to do with a splint or cast that is placed around a broken bone, or a bandage that covers a wound while it heals. The purpose of binding an injury is to provide a safe place for healing to occur.

God is that safe place for your heart. The healing might take time, but God is with you throughout the process, supporting you, sustaining you, protecting you, insulating you from further harm.

Will you choose to trust God with the broken pieces of your heart? It may not have been your choice or your fault that your heart was shattered, but you do have a choice in how you respond. You get to choose what to do from here.

To help you get started, I'd like to look at four ways to handle heartbreak. These are either/or responses. That is, each one has two contrasting terms that describe a choice you can make that will move you closer to or farther away from healing.

In the journey toward healing, you can't take two paths at once. Either you choose the road that leads toward healing for your soul, or you choose the road that might seem to keep your heart safe but inevitably leads toward an ever-smaller, ever-more-defensive world. God is your healer, and you will come out stronger than ever if you entrust your heart to him.

RECOGNIZE OR RATIONALIZE

The first choice you have when handling heartbreak is to *recognize* the pain or to *rationalize* denial or other unhealthy responses.

The first acknowledges that things are not what they need to be, while the second makes excuses. Denial evades reality. It dodges the truth in an effort to sweep things under the carpet and hope they go away.

Are you honest with your feelings? With your anger? With your pain? With your mistakes, your loss, your hurt? Or are you trying to pretend everything is fine when it's not? Not only is it honest to recognize where you are at emotionally and mentally, it's an essential step toward healing.

Have you ever known someone who just ended a five-year relationship, and two days later, they're telling everyone, "I'm good, I'm fine, I'm just moving on"?

And you're thinking, You don't look fine. You don't act fine. I've known you forever, and you are most definitely not okay.

They might be saying the right things, but anyone close to them can tell that their heart has been broken. They need time to recover. But if they refuse to admit they are hurt, how will they ever heal?

Maybe you've done this. Maybe you're still dealing with some level of heartbreak that was never fully healed, but you've convinced yourself that if you deny the problem, it will go away. If you call it by some other name, if you minimize it, if you make jokes about it, if you distract yourself from it, somehow it will heal itself. But just because you avoid something doesn't stop it from actually being there.

Even worse, if you never heal from what hurts you, you'll bleed on people who never cut you. You'll carry your wounds into other relationships where they can subtly affect how you see yourself, others, God, love, and life.

When it comes to relational heartbreak, you can't ignore it and you can't go around it. You have to face it. You have to walk through it. You have to be healed.

Don't claim it's all good when it's not. Don't rush your healing. Don't lie about your pain, whether to others or yourself. Remember, your pain is likely obvious to everyone around you. Your friends and family know you better than you might think.

Imagine breaking your leg and then walking into a room full of people, dragging your leg behind you, maybe dripping blood behind you, and smiling at everyone. "Hey, guys, I'm good. All good. Nothing to see here."

"Man, you're bleeding!"

"No, I'm not."

"Yes, you are. And your leg is bent funny."

"Nah, it's just a flesh wound."

I remember one time my dad was trying to hammer something when he missed and smashed his pointer finger. It was bad. He needed to go to the doctor. He needed someone to bind up the broken bones. But he refused to go. The finger did heal over time, but if you see his finger today, it's clearly bent. It never healed right.

So, yes, if you ignore your wound long enough, it might heal. Just because it heals on the outside doesn't mean that it healed properly, though. You can end up with crooked places and scar tissue that could have been avoided if you'd dealt with things directly from the beginning.

Sometimes rationalization goes beyond denial and becomes self-blame. In a weird way, you try to excuse or normalize the trauma by telling yourself that it's your fault. "I caused this problem. My heart is broken, but it's my fault. This is my new reality. I brought this on myself."

Even if you are to blame, that doesn't mean you don't need help or can't find healing. Regardless of how you got into this state, it's essential to be honest about the pain. Face the problem. Don't continue to rationalize the trauma away. Don't deny the fact that you're bleeding on everybody you come in contact with.

You may need outside help to heal your heart, just as you'd need a doctor to help with an injury. That help begins with Jesus, of course. He's the greatest healer of all. But it might also include therapy, counseling, opening up with close friends, or other methods of getting back on track. There is no shame in seeking help.

Choose to recognize your reality, then seek healing in your heartbreak.

RESOLVE OR RESIGN

Once you've recognized what has happened and how it's affecting you, your next choice is whether to *resolve* to improve your future or to *resign* yourself to your current situation.

Resolve refers to a firm commitment to a chosen path. It means you look at the course of healing before you and decide to stick with it, even if you don't see changes overnight.

If you feel deeply broken, the recovery process can seem as if it's too long, too difficult. You might start well—with prayer, self-care, emotional awareness, repentance, personal growth, worship, self-discipline—but then weeks and maybe even months pass, and the pain is still there.

At some point, you'll be tempted to give up on the new course of life you've set for yourself and turn toward some quick fix just to feel better. Maybe it's another toxic relationship. Maybe it's alcohol. Maybe it's eating, or shopping, or hours of self-pity. If unchecked, quick fixes can turn into escapism, addiction, or other forms of self-harm that only prolong the suffering.

Pain is a terrible thing to live with, but you have to have a realistic understanding of how long it takes for pain to go away, for healing to come, and for new life to flourish. If you're recovering from a years-long relationship of emotional or physical abuse, you won't get healthy overnight. If you've been wounded by someone who cheated on you, it could take a while before you can trust people again.

My wife, DawnCheré, grew up in a family of athletes. Her dad played professional sports and several of her five brothers were quarterbacks. They have seen some pretty nasty injuries. Maybe that's where the queasiness comes from, now that I think of it. The other day, my brother-in-law, Dakota, was sitting next to me, and he kept popping his shoulder in and out. I couldn't take it. "Can you stop?" I said. "I know it doesn't hurt you, but it hurts me just to hear it." David Dee, another one of my brother-in-laws, had two knee surgeries before he even graduated from high school. So I've seen them walk through severe injuries that have taken months, not just days or weeks, of recovery.

If an injury occurred on a Friday night, we wouldn't wake up Saturday morning and say to the injured family member, "Okay, take off that cast! You're ready. You got this. Come on, mind over matter, positive thinking, have some faith." We would never dream of doing that. Why? Because the guy was injured. He had a literal broken bone.

Why do we give space for the physical healing process but think we should be able to pull all the pieces together overnight when our hearts are broken? It doesn't work that fast, but that doesn't mean God has abandoned us or that healing is not taking place. God is in the midst of the broken pieces, but we have to keep trusting him. We have to let him bind our wounds.

Healing—complete healing—is not a quick fix. It is choosing to trust God day after day as he thoroughly and wholly mends your heart. God wants to lead you toward restoration and strength. Will you choose to have resolve? Will you walk steadily down the path God has placed in front of you?

Healing—complete healing—is not a quick fix. It is choosing to trust God day after day as he thoroughly and wholly mends your heart. God wants to lead you toward restoration and strength.

REBUILD OR REACT

The third choice you have is whether to *rebuild* or *react*. Rebuilding looks toward the future. When you choose to rebuild, you take steps toward a better, brighter, healthier you. On the other hand, when you choose to react, you look toward the past and become fixated on the present. Reacting is a knee-jerk response that is incapable of building for tomorrow because it's all about pain avoidance and self-protection.

Returning to the metaphor of binding up a broken bone: a cast is designed to immobilize the bone, holding it in place while it heals. Not only does it realign and reset the bone, but it also restricts the arm or leg from hurting itself further while the healing process happens.

That principle of restriction for realignment applies to our hearts as well. One of the most common mistakes people make when they get out of a bad relationship is to jump right back into another bad relationship. It's often an attempt to blunt the pain, but it only prolongs or increases suffering. You can't escape pain by creating more pain. You can't fill the holes in your heart with one-night stands or shallow romance.

Sure, for a moment, these things might mask those dark emotions. But in reality, all you're doing is reacting, not rebuilding. If you keep moving on to the *next* thing without dealing with the *previous* thing, your heart will never be rebuilt. Instead, it will go from wound to wound, from pain to pain, from drama to drama.

Restrict yourself.

Let yourself heal.

Give your mind, will, emotions, and spirit space to rebuild.

Giving your soul time to rebuild itself doesn't mean checking out of life, though. Every time DC's brothers ended up with another random appendage encased in a cast, they needed to be immobile for a day or two, but then they'd have to get up and start living life again, even if that meant using a crutch. They didn't hit the football field, of course—but they also didn't spend three months sipping Capri Sun pouches and channel surfing from the couch.

Why? Because lack of activity is almost as bad for your body as too much activity or inappropriate activity. While my brother-in-laws were in recovery, doctors always focused on two things: intake and output. They gave specific instructions about what food and medicine they should consume (intake) and what exercises they should do and how to do them (output). Both are necessary for healthy bone growth and healing.

Your heart needs the same two things while it is healing. Let's think about your intake for a moment. If you're going through a season of heartbreak, what you consume matters. I'm not talking about chocolate or other comfort food (calories don't count after breakups). I'm talking about what you feed your soul. What should that include?

Maybe the most obvious thing you should be filling your heart, soul, and mind with is God's Word. His truth, his way of thinking, and his value system needs to become part of you. That means you have to read it and let it take root in your heart. It's not enough to put a quote from God's Word up on your refrigerator or Instagram feed; you have to get it inside you. That's where it begins to do its healing. That's where it starts to work.

Second, fill yourself with *healthy perspectives about relationships.* There's nothing like heartbreak to make you question everything. That's good. It's smart to evaluate yourself, your values, your habits, your goals.

A healthy perspective starts by recognizing that people cannot complete you. If that's your aim in a relationship, you're going to be disappointed because people can't satisfy you. They can sharpen you, but there's only one person who can satisfy you, and his name is Jesus. It's easy to forget that when life is going well and you are madly in love with the man or woman of your dreams. But heartbreak has a way of reminding you that your hope is in Jesus, not a mate. Don't look for someone who completes you: look for someone who sharpens you, who walks with you, who shares life with you.

Third, fill yourself with *a realistic vision for a romantic relationship.* We talked about vision earlier when we looked at our tendency to fall in love with fairy tales, so I won't repeat myself here. Just remember that when things fall apart, you can always learn something. You can polish and tweak and expand your understanding of what you're seeking. Sometimes you have to see what you *don't* want before you realize what you *do* want. And sometimes you have to go through some pain before you're willing to look inward and see if there are things you need to change about yourself. Whether you learn more about yourself, about what you want, or about people in general, breakups can shape your vision for the future in a positive way. They can make you a wiser, better, bigger person who won't make the same mistakes twice.

Finally, *fill yourself with grace.* Yes, you need to be honest about your own mistakes and weaknesses, but that doesn't mean you live under a cloud of guilt and shame. Give yourself grace and space to recover. Honestly, it will help you be nicer to other people too, and that's always a good thing.

What goes into your heart is what will shape your life. That's why it is so important—especially in heartbreak—to make sure your intake is healthy. Protect what you allow into your heart.

One of my favorite scriptures was written by King Solomon: "Above all else, guard your heart, for everything you do flows from it" (Proverbs 4:23). He was one of the wisest people who ever lived. So when he says, "above all else," it carries a lot of weight. It's like he's telling us, "I've said a lot of good things in this book. If you weren't listening, okay, but hear this one thing."

Solomon was saying that your heart is the very essence

of who you are. It is the intangible seat of your soul, that inner place from which you make all of your decisions, the source of your feelings, the voice that guides your thoughts, the force that directs your actions. It must be kept healthy.

The most secure area of a bank is the vault. If tomorrow you got a job at a bank, it's highly unlikely they'd give you vault-level security clearance on day one. Why? Because they don't know you. They have to watch you for a while. They have to see your track record. If you prove yourself worthy of trust, day after day, you might be given security clearance if your duties warrant it. Why? Because the vault is the greatest asset of the bank. It is where the most valuable treasures are kept.

Think of your heart as the greatest asset of your life. It's the location of your most valuable treasures: your confidence, your identity, your dreams. Maybe you've given security clearance to things and people who have no business getting near your heart. You need to learn how to guard that treasure vault because if you don't, things get in it that shouldn't be there, and they affect everything. Solomon said, "everything you do flows from it." What gets into your heart determines what comes out of it. You have to resolve in your spirit, "I'm going to guard my heart."

> *Shame* should not have keys to your heart.
> *Doubt* should not have keys to your heart.
> *Fear* should not have keys to your heart.
> *Depression* should not have keys to your heart.
> *Loneliness* should not have keys to your heart.
> *Bitterness* should not have keys to your heart.
> *Hatred* should not have keys to your heart.
> *Anxiety* should not have keys to your heart.

Sure, you'll feel those things from time to time. That's normal. They're like visitors to the vault of your heart, though. They don't work there. They don't have unquestioned access. They can't come and go as they please. They don't get to walk around unaccompanied. They aren't allowed to take things and leave things and move things around inside your soul. And at any moment, you can usher them out and lock the door. Your heart is too precious to allow just anything or anyone to come inside.

When your heart is broken, your intake matters, as we've seen. That's not all, though. Your output is just as important. Healing a broken heart is not just about receiving, but also about giving. This is where people often fail to respond correctly because getting hurt, well, it hurts. Badly. And pain makes us turn inward. It makes us hesitant to step out. We think action will mean more pain, and we don't think we can take any more pain.

If you've ever broken a bone, though, you know that doctors want you to move as much as you safely can from day one. They know that your muscles will atrophy and suffer even more if you give in to the fear of getting hurt again. Your blood needs to circulate, and your muscles need to stay active so your body can rebuild itself properly.

Your heart might be broken, but that doesn't mean *you* are broken. And it doesn't mean you have to break off the things around you that are giving you life. Don't shut down, give up, or check out. You need output. You need activity. You need to keep giving and loving and serving other people.

Specifically, stay in community. Don't take a break from people who love and care for you just because one person you trusted hurt you deeply. You need people around you. We all do. Don't let the person who didn't love you keep you away from the people who do love you. Don't let them stop you from meeting the person who *will* love you.

The devil would love nothing more than to isolate you, to make you withdrawn, self-protected, hidden inside a shell made of hurt and hate, untouchable and unreachable in an attempt to be unhurtable. He wants to lead you into the dark valley of the soul, and then convince you to make your home there. *Nobody understands me,* you might think. *Nobody knows how badly my heart is broken. I'm going to do life alone. I'm never trusting anyone again.*

That is a natural reaction, but remember, you can choose to rebuild, not react. If you're going to rebuild, you'll need people around you. You'll have to trust again and love again.

There is an amazing woman on our church volunteer team named Jen. Jen helped us start the church, and she oversees our load-in and our load-out teams at our rented church locations. Keep in mind, these are not easy areas to serve in. The work starts at 5:45 a.m. and ends at 11:00 p.m., and there is a lot of physical labor involved and zero applause and glory. There is a special place in heaven for load-in and load-out volunteers, I'm sure of it.

Anyway, Jen broke her foot a while back. Before church, I was out in the courtyard of our location when I saw Jen. She had a massive cast and boot on her foot. But she was still walking around, directing the load-in team. "Take this over there. Bring that over here. Come on now, let's go!"

If there were ever a moment to skip load-in and load-out, if there were ever a valid excuse, it would be a broken foot in a cast. As I watched her leading and serving with her foot stuck out in front of her, I realized something. Even when some things are broken, there are other things you can do. Brokenness does not mean you have to stop doing what you want to do and being who you were made to be. It cannot hold you back from your calling or from allowing love to fill your heart.

If you have a broken heart, you can still worship God. You can still serve him. You can still find a community of people to surround you. You can still love and give to others. You can still let the peace of Jesus dwell inside your soul. You can still dream about the future.

Even in the middle of heartbreak, you can still choose to rebuild.

→ If you have a broken heart.

RESTORE OR RELAPSE

The fourth and final choice you face when your heart is hurting is whether to *restore or to relapse*. To be restored means to receive what you once had, to return to a place you once occupied. Restored refers to *rising again*. Relapse, on the other hand, means *falling again*. It is about returning to a negative place or reliving a cycle of defeat or failure.

When dealing with a broken heart, you must trust that God is at work to restore you, even if you can't see him. He is binding your wounds and healing your hurt. If you can't trust God to restore you, then you're left attempting to pull things together on your own. That often results in falling back into the same pit, making the same mistakes, reliving the same defeat.

In other words, if you aren't *restored by God*, you'll tend to *relapse by yourself*.

That's not necessarily a reflection on you. I'm not saying that you should have been smarter or tried harder or worked harder. I'm saying you weren't designed to do this life alone. You need God.

Earlier, we talked about God binding our wounds. The word "bind" has another use in the Bible, though, one that carries deep, beautiful significance. To bind is to enter into a covenant. Sometimes people speak of contracts as being binding, and that's the idea behind a covenant—two parties link themselves together through a voluntary agreement. Their covenant is a shared bond that unites them with mutual commitments and promises.

Throughout the Bible, we see God establishing covenants with his people. He agreed to bind himself to us. To fulfill his promises to us. To be faithful to us forever.

A covenant is not the same as a contract. A contract is

based on what you get, but a covenant is based on what you give. Covenant is based on relationship, commitment, and sacrifice. God's covenant is an exchange of love and life between humanity and God himself.

The covenant we enjoy today was established by Jesus through his life, death, and resurrection. It is often called the "new covenant," and it's the gospel. The good news of salvation in Jesus. But the gospel is more than just a doctrinal statement or a theological framework. It's a relationship based on promises made by God himself, who can never lie, who will never change his mind, who will always keep his word.

Two thousand years ago, Jesus came as a baby. He lived thirty-three years here on this planet. He led a perfect, sinless life. Then he chose to give up his life for you and me. The night before his death, Jesus told his disciples that his spilled blood was the sign of a new covenant between God and humanity. It was a covenant made in Jesus' death, but it was proven by his resurrected life, showing once and for all that Jesus has power not only over sin but over death itself.

That is the God we serve. That is the Jesus who promised to love us and to be with us forever. Jesus was bruised, beaten, and broken for us. And he was raised to new life for us as well. He knows how to heal the broken because he was broken. He knows how to put the pieces of your heart back together because he is the author of life itself. Jesus sees you in your pain because he has been to the grave and back, and he triumphed over it all: and now he lives to love and aid you.

God's love is binding. It is the agreement that holds you close to him. Sin has no claim over you. Anxiety has no hold over you. Fear has no power over you. When the broken pieces of your heart seem impossible to heal, God himself intervenes.

If Jesus could love you so much that he gave his life for you before you even knew him, when humanity was still lost in sin, doesn't it stand to reason that he is more committed to you now than ever? Now that you are seeking him, trusting him, following him? The apostle Paul said it this way: "For if, while we were God's enemies, we were reconciled to him through the death of his Son, how much more, having been reconciled, shall we be saved through his life!" (Romans 5:10).

You are covered and protected. God has bound up your wounds, but he has also bound you to himself. His covenant will not change with the seasons. It does not waiver based upon your attitude or your mood or your emotions or your failures or your successes. This covenant is sure and secure. It is a foundation on which you can build your life, and the storms, winds, and rain will not make you fall.

Will you choose to allow the hands of God to restore you, or will you risk relapse by continuing to try to keep things together on your own? It's up to you. God is close to you, and he's offering to help. He is the great restorer.

I was given a Bible when I graduated from college in 2007, and it became the Bible I read and preached from for many years. I'm the kind of person who thinks the Bible should be highlighted, marked up, written in, and engaged with. I know some people believe the Bible deserves so much respect that you shouldn't write in it, but I think it deserves so much respect that you should devour it. You should make it yours, take it to heart, study it until the words jump off the page and the pages fall out of the book. I think the messier your Bible is, the better your life is!

Anyway, my Bible started falling apart after a while. The cover cracked, flaked, and eventually fell off, the pages were barely hanging onto the spine—it was a mess. But I loved that Bible.

One day, as a gift, DawnCheré sent it away to be restored. The pages had to be reattached to the spine and it needed a new cover. That is fascinating to me: you never think about the spine, but it's what holds all the pages together. Do you know what that whole restorative process is called?

Rebinding.

In order for my Bible to be restored, it had to be rebound.

If you are going through heartache, your knee-jerk reaction might be this: "My heart is broken, and I'm hurting. What I need is a rebound relationship."

No, you don't need a *re*-bound relationship; you need to be re-*bound* to God. You need to be repaired, recovered, restored by him.

The cross of Jesus is much like the spine of a book. It's what holds us all together: the pieces and pages of our lives are bound to him in love and grace. Let the covenant love that Jesus showed on the cross become the strength of your life. Allow it to bring restoration to the dangling pages of your heart.

When you surrender your heart, God doesn't throw the pages away. He doesn't look at you and say, "He's a lost cause. There's no hope for her. I'd be better off starting over."

He embraces you where you are, and he restores you. He rebinds you in him. He takes your mistakes, your shame, your embarrassing moments, and your regrets, and he binds those moments together with grace until your entire life is a story of triumph for the world to read.

Choose to let God rebind, recover, and reglue your life together in him. He is the great restorer, and you are safe in his hands.

***

I love this quote by author James Sherman: "You can't go back and change the beginning, but you can start where you are and change the ending."[15] You can't undo the past, and that's okay—you don't live there anyway. Today is what matters, and tomorrow, and the day after that.

Yes, the pain is real, and it can feel overwhelming. But pain is not the author of your story, nor does it have to be the end of your story. The healing process has begun. Your heart will be whole again because God is with you. Not to condemn you, not to criticize you, not to rush you, but to hold you and to heal you.

Together with God, you are changing your ending, starting today.

Together with God.

JAMILA'S STORY

Heartbreak is hard. Every time I got into a relationship, I would tell myself that I would not allow my heart to be broken again. But every time, it would get broken again. In the past three years, I have had my heart broken twice. After the first time, I was extremely bitter and resentful. I didn't want to recognize the heartbreak and instead brushed it off. As a key leader in our church, I never wanted to seem to be struggling with something.

A few months later, I found myself dating a different friend, which eventually turned into a relationship. There were so many things from my previous relationship that bled into my new one. My insecurities were still there. My trust issues were still there. Although I thought that I was jumping into this relationship differently, there were things that I ignored. I just wanted to be with someone who I thought was the one for me.

I didn't give myself time to heal. I didn't give myself time to recognize my faults and the areas I needed to work on in myself. Six months after I officially got into this new relationship, we broke up. However, I again didn't give myself time to heal. A month later, I ended up jumping back into this relationship without taking time to process and recognize things that needed to be addressed.

Then, it happened again. I found myself experiencing heartbreak just two months later. Pastor Rich mentioned once that insanity is doing the same thing over and over again and expecting different results. This time I knew I had to do something different. I realized I needed to stay in community to handle this heartbreak. I opened up to trustworthy friends about my situation and how I was feeling instead of suppressing it all. Being surrounded by people who supported me and reminded me of my calling truly helped me in that season.

In addition to staying in community, I took time to be honest with myself. I took time to recognize my heartbreak, and I resolved to improve my future. I took steps toward a better, brighter, healthier me. I started counseling to talk through some of my feelings and thoughts. I even started to work out more and eat healthier.

Looking back, I realized that I didn't handle heartbreak well. I would suppress my feelings to look like a "strong leader." I would move on to the next thing in order to distract myself from reality and what I needed to work on in myself. However, God has been so good to me through each and every moment. He is the only one who can truly heal my heartbreak when I surrender my feelings, hurt, and thoughts to him.

09
DEHY-
DRATED
DATING

dating ♡

HAVE YOU EVER BEEN IN A SITUATION where your eyes played tricks on you? Maybe you were alone at home late at night, and suddenly you were sure you saw something move in the shadows of your living room. Before you could decide whether to run, scream, or dial 911, you realized it was just a tree casting weird shadows, or your cat jumping in through an open window, or a curtain blowing in the wind like some low-budget horror movie. Instantly your terror turns to embarrassment. How did you let your mind get so carried away?

Being alone at night has a way of awakening your imagination and creating ghosts out of shadows. That's not the only thing that can cause a distorted view of reality, though. Exhaustion, fear, hunger, thirst, anger, and loneliness—to name just a few—can make us see things that aren't there or miss what is in plain sight.

As humans, we have to understand our perceptions are fallible. Perhaps nowhere is that more important than when you are pursuing a romantic relationship with someone you could spend the rest of your life with. Why? Because the last thing you want is to find out too late that the person you fell in love with doesn't exist. That you made them up, that you saw them as what you wanted them to be instead of seeing them as they are, that you turned a blind eye to reality and instead fell in love with a fantasy.

Try telling that to your brain, though, when you're falling in love. Lovers are hardly known for their critical thinking skills. Just think about the terms often used to describe a person in the thralls of romantic love. They are *bewitched, enchanted, infatuated, swept off their feet, madly in love, hopelessly in love, head over heels, lovestruck, lovesick.*

None of these terms convey logical or rational behavior—quite the opposite. They stress the out-of-control, caught-up-in-the-moment nature of romantic love. Trying to be rational in love is like trying to do math equations while you're riding a roller coaster. It's not going to happen. The rush of emotions, the newness, the risk, the flirting, the hormones, the uncertainty, the frantic attempts to figure out the other person's intentions and feelings—love is not a logical endeavor.

That's half the fun, though, right? Nobody wants to turn love into some logical, transactional, boring experience.

And yet, you have to be wise. You must be self-aware. You need emotional intelligence and patience. You have to think about the future. You must pay attention and walk carefully. You can't move too fast, but you can't move too slow, either. You can't seem too desperate, but you can't seem uninterested, either.

In other words, love is both out of your control and within your control at the same time.

That's a lot to navigate. A lot to think about. But that's dating for you. You have to fall in love without losing your head. You have to give away your heart without getting it broken in the process. How do you do that?

Here's one important piece of advice.

Don't date thirsty.

I'm not talking about your actual state of hydration here, although I hope you're drinking enough water. I'm also not hinting at how many drinks you should or shouldn't consume on a date (but if I were, I'd tell you to be careful because you need your wits about you).

That's not what I mean by thirsty.

Thirsty means desperate. It means unsatisfied. It means urgently wanting something, including—but not limited to—sex.

To date thirsty is to date from a place of desperation. That won't end well because your mental or emotional state will blind you. Your eyes, metaphorically speaking, will play tricks on you.

Thirst has a way of making us believe things that aren't real. I'm sure you've seen those cliché movie scenes: a lost, thirsty traveler is dragging himself across the desert. He lifts his desperate gaze and sees an oasis of palm trees, pools and ice-cold beverages in the distance. It isn't real, of course, but he thinks it is. He runs toward it and dives into a pool, expecting to satisfy his thirst, only to end up spitting out sand, more dehydrated than ever. The dehydration didn't cause the mirage; heat waves did. But it made the guy more likely to believe them because he was desperate for what he hoped he saw to be real.

If you date thirsty, you'll start seeing and believing things that aren't real. Your perspective will be skewed because your thoughts, motives, desires, or emotions are not in a healthy place. I've seen it again and again. The people who seem to have the most breakups, the deepest pain, the greatest drama and trauma, are the ones who date thirsty. They go into relationships like that desperate desert traveler, expecting it to be something it can never be. When it's over, they're left with nothing but a mouthful of sand.

And they're still thirsty.

WALK-AWAY POWER

power!

Not dating thirsty means *not expecting a relationship to complete you.* We talked about this in the first chapter. The burden of your happiness is too much weight for any human to carry. If you are not in a healthy place emotionally, if you're desperate for a person to ease your pain—or heal your hurt, or fill your heart, or give you value—you'll end up chasing mirages and diving into sand dunes. Finding your satisfaction in God, not in a significant other, is a much better way to date. It frees you up to relate to other people from a place of inner peace and self-confidence.

Financial experts say that when you're negotiating a deal, you need walk-away power. That means whether you're buying a used car or brokering a multi-million-dollar merger, you have to be willing to walk away if the deal isn't what you want or deserve.

How much more necessary is that advice when you're getting to know a possible future spouse? In dating and love, there is a time to give away your heart. But it's probably not on the first date. Or the second. There is only one thing that will give you healthy walk-away power: the inner security that comes from being complete in God.

Of course, you're not looking for the best "deal" when dating, so don't push the metaphor too far. But you do want to avoid getting yourself into something you'll both regret. That means you must be able to objectively look at your relationship and decide what is healthy and right.

I said it earlier: you shouldn't rush love. Let it develop naturally by genuinely getting to know the person you are starting to fall for. Get to know them on a realistic timeline, without pressuring things to move faster than they should out of an inner need to be validated or the fear that you'll lose the person. Be willing to walk away if you see red flags. As your connection increases and trust grows, you'll reveal your hearts to each other, one layer at a time. You'll share your dreams, fears, pain, doubts, goals, quirks, tastes, values, thoughts, and hopes with each other.

That means talking.

Lots of talking.

Talking is not something you do while you wait to see if you're going to fall in love. It is an essential part of falling in love. Anyone can hold hands or make out, but not everyone can talk maturely about difficult subjects. Communication, not cuddling, is the road to intimacy. This is the only way to know someone fully, and you can't *love* someone well until you *know* them well.

LOTS!

YOU MIGHT BE THIRSTY IF...

Have you ever had a friend give you the absolute craziest reasons for why they are staying with someone? It's obvious to you that their relationship is doomed for disaster, but your friend won't listen to reason. "I know we're right for each other because we have a special song. Whenever we listen to that song together, it just feels right. I can't explain it."

Well, it's great that your music tastes are compatible. But a special song is not love. Start a Spotify playlist together. Start a band, even. But don't start a family. Not yet.

What does dating thirsty look like? Glad you asked. You might be thirsty if:

- You care more about how you look than who you are.
- You care more about being wanted than respected.
- You don't stop texting her even when you never get a reply.
- You continue to pursue him even though he's never pursued you.
- Your feelings overrule your faith.
- That special somebody's voice outweighs everyone else's voice, including your own.
- You invite him to your house, but you can't invite him to your church.
- You can take her to the movies, but you can't take her to meet your mother.
- You spend more time on Tinder than you do reading your Bible.
- You change your relationship status on social media to "whatever you say it is."
- You used to want a man who carried his cross, but you're falling for a man with a tattoo of a cross.

- You used to want somebody who would build God's house, but now you'll settle for a man who at least doesn't live at his parent's house.
- You used to want someone who prayed in Jesus' name, but now you're dating someone who curses with Jesus' name.
- You used to serve on the down-low; now you creep on the down-low.
- You're a guy who only signs up to serve at your church once a year, and it's at the women's conference.
- You'll only offer to pray for someone if she's pretty.
- You get jealous when another guy talks to the girl you like, even when it's a seating host just doing his job.
- You don't care that his divorce hasn't been finalized.
- You are willing to date your best friend's ex.
- You flirt to convert.
- You are sure God has told you to marry her—but God hasn't informed her.

That's just a sample list. A starter pack for thirsty singles. My guess is you could add a few more to it if you tried. Just think back to the dates that went bad or the creeps you blocked from your DMs. We all recognize thirsty people when they are trying to use us, but we aren't so good at spotting the thirst in our own souls.

The Bible has a lot to say about thirst. One passage that comes to mind describes a conversation between two thirsty people standing beside a well. One was Jesus, and the other was a Samaritan woman who was there to draw water. They definitely weren't dating, though. Jesus was physically thirsty: he asked the woman for a drink of water, which is how their conversation began. The woman, however, was emotionally and spiritually thirsty, as we see in their discussion.

The woman had been married five times and was now living with a man who was not her husband. She was probably alone at the well in the heat of the day because she wanted to avoid the stares and gossip of the other townspeople who came to the well in the cool of the morning. As the conversation with Jesus unfolded, he didn't condemn her for the broken marriages. Instead, he pointed her to the only thing that could satisfy her: the love of God.

He told her, "If you knew the gift of God and who it is that asks you for a drink, you would have asked him and he would have given you living water" (John 4:10). In other words, the woman didn't need another human relationship to bring her happiness. She needed God. She needed to find completion and wholeness in the grace of Jesus.

By the end of the story, this woman who had gone alone and thirsty to the well left with her thirst quenched, and then returned with the entire town following her. She became the mouthpiece of Jesus for her village. Once she saw Jesus for who he was, she became who she was meant to be. She thought she needed the love of a man, but she needed the love of God.

It's the same for you and me.

In the Bible, the number seven often symbolizes completion or divine perfection. Interestingly, Jesus was the seventh man in the Samaritan woman's life. She had searched for happiness with six different men, but she never found it—until she met Jesus. There's a lesson there for us: no romantic relationship could ever fill the role of God in our hearts.

Finding yourself in the love of God is the best preparation for finding yourself in love with another human being. You can't expect another person to give you what only God can provide. You can't demand that someone else do for you what only God can do. On the other hand, don't expect someone else to do what you alone can do. Remember, it's your party. It's up to you to make the most of your life and relationships. Be secure in who you are and where you are, and take responsibility for your life going forward.

Avoid both extremes. Don't try to find a man or a woman

who will take the place of God—that's called idolatry. And don't find someone to take the place of yourself—that's called identity theft. Neither God nor that special someone is going to miraculously do what you were created to do, and that's a good thing because it means you have full right and control over your body and life.

Trust God.

Find your value in him.

Believe his love.

Own your journey.

Be secure in who you are.

Then, from that stable platform of healthy self-esteem, fall as head over heels in love as you want. Cannonball into love. Skydive into love. Nosedive, stagedive, or bellyflop into love, whatever works for you. If you know who you are, and if you are walking close to God, love will be the greatest adventure of your life.

There are a lot of books out there that talk about dating and romance, so I won't cover everything that could be said about these topics in one chapter. If you're interested in learning more, I highly recommend my friend Michael Todd's book, *Relationship Goals,* to start with, and there are others as well.

I'd also recommend talking to a few couples whose romance or marriage could be described as relationship goals for you. Ask them how they did it. What they learned. What they would do differently. You'll find a lot of different answers because there is no magic formula. There is only wisdom, love, risk, faith, and patience. What works for one person isn't necessarily what works for another, but you can learn from all of it.

What I don't recommend, though, is just going with the flow and doing what everyone else is doing. Why? Because there are a lot of thirsty people out there, and they don't have answers, either. The people who give you the loudest advice often have the longest trail of broken relationships behind them.

Thirst can be caused by many things, not just overactive hormones. So, in the interest of avoiding dehydrated dating, I'm

TRUST!

TRUST GOD!

TRUST God.

Trust God.

TRUST GOD.

Find your value in him.
Believe his love.
Own your journey.
Be secure in who you are.

going to share a few thoughts about dating. Specifically, the past, the future, and the present, in that order, because each of these three things can have a major impact on your dating experience.

HEAL FROM THE PAST

A healthy dating experience requires that you find healing from past pain. I don't mean forgetting the past, because you can't. I just mean learning from it and then moving on.

Keep in mind, there's a fine line between *learning* from the past and being *traumatized* by the past. You might still be trying to find that line. I think we all are, to be honest. Being human is messy. Growing up is difficult. Relating to imperfect people causes scars and wounds. I don't think it's realistic, therefore, to expect to go into a new romantic relationship unscathed from the past; or to expect your partner to be perfectly whole, either. Love heals and covers, after all, and true love can bring healing to past trauma.

Having said that, though, you want to make things as easy on love as possible, so deal with as much of your trauma as you can now. I don't say that flippantly, either. There might be significant issues to deal with, and that requires bravery and perseverance. You'll come out stronger on the other side, though, and more at peace. Whether or not you end up getting married, you can only benefit from dealing with the ghosts of your past, particularly unresolved childhood issues or trust issues.

Unresolved Childhood Issues

Desperation can be a result of pain and abandonment experienced early in life. Having "daddy issues" is a real thing, and it doesn't affect just women. Take seriously the experiences that hurt you when you were younger, and find healing now.

If you don't, you'll inevitably try to use intimacy to heal wounds that are too big, too deep, and too hidden for a loved one to heal. Unless you're dating a psychologist or a therapist (and even if you are), they probably won't be up to the task of putting the pieces of your childhood back together.

Who is up to it? God, of course. And you. And time. And likely a therapist you aren't dating. All working together to restore what should never have been taken from you in the first place. But it was—and now it's up to you to bring closure to those things so you can step into a better future.

Trust Issues

Maybe your desperation doesn't come from your childhood relationships as much as it does from your adult ones. You've been betrayed, hurt or abandoned, and you vowed you'd never let it happen again.

That's an understandable vow to take, but it's not one you can keep. You can't guarantee your heart will never be broken again. Yes, you must be careful about how quickly you give it away, but you also have to restore your faith in humanity and allow yourself to be vulnerable again.

This means dealing with trust issues. You can't love well with a heart that's still bleeding. If you try, you'll project past hurt onto present relationships. You'll see ghosts everywhere, even if they're just cats jumping through windows or curtains blowing in the wind. "He's going to cheat on me, I know it. Guys always cheat." "She is talking to another guy. That's how it started last time." Without even realizing it, you're punishing one person for the sins of another. You're pushing them away because someone else did you wrong.

Again, I'm no therapist, so I'm not presenting an exhaustive list of the past issues that might be affecting you in the present. I have learned, though, that God is the best healer of all. He's the best counselor, the best confidante, the best friend you could have. I don't say that to minimize the role of professionals, but rather to encourage you to pay attention to the still, small voice inside you that is healing your heart and rebuilding your self-esteem. The closer you draw to God, the more he will repair the wounds in your soul. He sees them better than anyone, and he cares for you more than everyone. Lean into the restoring power of the Holy Spirit.

PREPARE FOR THE FUTURE

Healing the known pain of the past is one thing, but how do you prepare for the unknowns of the future? Short answer: do your best and be ready to pivot. Even though you can't fully predict the future, thinking about it and planning for it gives direction and purpose to today.

One of the tendencies of youth is to treat life like it will last forever; to live as if today didn't matter because there are an infinite number of tomorrows. Tomorrow comes quickly, though. And trust me, marriage and kids (especially kids) change everything. For the better, of course. But also for the, well, I'm not going to fill in that blank. Let's just say you'll never have more free time, more liberty, or more energy than you do now.

You think you're stressed now? You think you're busy now? You think life is expensive now? You think you deal with a lot of expectations now? You think it's hard to get out of bed now? You think your to-do list is long now?

(Cue slow, evil laugh).

Just wait until you're married and have kids.

I wouldn't trade it for the world, though. Neither should you. Both God's grace and your capacity grow as you go, so don't be too worried about the pressures to come. You'll be fine.

My point, though, is that you shouldn't be complacent now. You'll be glad later for whatever you can accomplish in this season of singleness. Here are three ways you can prepare for the future.

Get Out of Debt

This can be a tough one, especially if you're carrying thousands of dollars in student loans or consumer debt. That burden will only get heavier if your future partner also has debt. The last thing I want is to make you feel guilty if you are struggling to pay off what you owe. However, what I often see is the opposite, people who don't take their spending and their debts seriously enough now.

If your goal is marriage, kids, a house, a stable life, and eventual retirement, you're going to have to deal with money issues. Either that or marry for money. I guess that's an option. But assuming that's not the route you plan to take, or that you don't have any wealthy suitors knocking at your door with flowers and a ring, you need to learn about paying off debt, balancing a budget, spending wisely, and saving for the future.

That's not easy, but it's not impossible, either. There are many sources of information and strategies to achieve financial freedom, but you have to put in the work to find and follow them. If you can go into marriage with no consumer debt and as little student debt as possible, you'll thank yourself for it later. And your spouse will, too.

Build Something

I've repeated this idea throughout this book: don't wait until you're married to start living. Start now. Build something now. I don't know what that looks like for you, but it likely includes one or more of the following.

Build your education.
Build your career.

Build your talents.
Build your financial picture.
Build your friendships.
Build your passion.
Build your ministry.
Build your physical health.
Build your inner health.
Build your generosity.
Build your life experiences.
Build your wisdom.
Build your character.
Build your influence.
Build your relationship with God.

You don't know how long you'll be single. That's not up to you. But you know what you have in your hands now. You know what opportunities lie before you today. You know what dreams stir your heart and what passions excite your soul.

Lean into those things. Build toward those things.

"Do not worry about tomorrow," Jesus said, "for tomorrow will worry about itself. Each day has enough trouble of its own" (Matthew 6:34). He wasn't being pessimistic (okay, maybe just a little); he was trying to get people to focus on the day at hand. It's all you have, after all.

Establish Healthy Habits

"Healthy habits" is a broad term, of course. I can't tell you what healthy looks like or what habits to focus on. That's up to you.

The idea of habit, though, is significant. Your brain can't consciously process the millions of decisions it handles every day, so most of them get outsourced to your subconscious. That's where habits come in. Habits are like pre-made decisions. They are templates for your brain to draw on when facing choices, so it doesn't have to interrupt you too much. After all, you're clearly busy right

You don’t know how long you’ll be single. That’s not up to you. But you know what you have in your hands now. You know what opportunities lie before you today.

YOU KNOW WHAT YOU HAVE.

now, watching season ten of some sitcom that came out in the nineties.

Habits aren't out of your control, but they aren't entirely under your control, either. When used correctly, they are a powerful force for good. When used poorly, they can derail the best intentions and the most promising lives. Here's how it works.

> Values determine your decisions.
> Decisions determine your actions.
> Actions determine your habits.
> Habits determine your future.

That's a little bit sobering. For example, your future health (or future death, if we are really being morbid) could be connected to your eating or exercise habits today. Your financial security when you retire in forty years could be determined by your spending habits today. Habits matter.

How does this affect dating and marriage? Well, the health of your future marriage could be influenced by your dating habits, relationship habits, and conflict resolution habits today. How you handle purity and temptation could affect your intimacy later. Whether you learn to communicate well and to forgive quickly will impact the health and even longevity of your marriage.

Don't be freaked out by this. Habits predict tendencies and influence probabilities, but they don't guarantee outcomes. I'm not saying you'll get a divorce just because you've had a couple of nasty breakups any more than I'm saying you'll get diabetes because you ate two doughnuts for breakfast.

If you're serious about setting up your marriage and family for success, take a good look at your lifestyle now. What habits should you develop? What habits should you tweak? What habits should you eliminate? If you retake control of the little decisions you've outsourced to those bad habits, you can literally change your future.

These three things—eliminating debt, building for the future, and establishing healthy habits—are just a few of the steps you could take now to prepare for the reality you want to live tomorrow.

Nobody can predict the future, but that's no excuse not to try, or not to hope, or not to prepare. Building a healthy, secure foundation now is an act of faith in God. Besides that, it's an indication of your loyalty and love toward a family you have yet to meet and a future you have yet to experience.

BE WISE IN THE PRESENT

Healing your past and preparing for your future are part of healthy dating, but if you're currently navigating the dating scene, your biggest questions are probably a lot more urgent than paying off student loans. You're wondering why dating is so expensive, or whether to swipe left or right, or how to know if she likes you, or how quickly to text back, or what he meant by that comment, or what she was saying with that facial expression, or how soon is too soon, or how much is too much.

Don't worry, I'm not going to tell you who to marry or how soon to hold hands. That's beyond my pay grade. Here are a four suggestions, though, based on countless conversations with dating couples over the years.

Postpone the Physical

We'll talk about this more in the next chapter, but the physical component is usually not too hard in a relationship. Humans are quick learners, and when it comes to touching, the learning curve is easy. And a lot of fun, to be honest. That's why being a good kisser is overrated—it doesn't take that long to learn, assuming you have decent dental hygiene and you're not a selfish jerk. The same goes for any physical expression of love, including sex.

As I mentioned before, though, getting physical can mask deeper problems. It can be tempting to "kiss and make up" rather than "talking and actually dealing with issues." Hormones can't fix toxic relationships, no matter what you see in the movies. But communication can. Humility can. A growth mindset can. Love can. And believe me, the physical intimacy that follows that level of soul intimacy is a whole different level. There's a reason make-up sex is its own category.

What is okay, and *when* is it okay in a relationship? That's not for me to determine. Sorry. The Bible is clear about the need to be pure, holy, honest, appropriate, and wise in all areas of life, including your sexuality. I'll get into that a little more in the next chapter. I will say this: Don't override any hesitancy of your partner. That is manipulation and abuse. Also, make sure everything you do is based on true love, a love that cares for and gives to the other, not a desire for self-gratification. Beyond that, it's up to the two of you to decide as you live out your faith and choices before God.

Don't Missionary Date

Missionary dating, a.k.a. the old flirt-to-convert strategy, is the idea that it's fine to date someone who isn't following Jesus because sooner or later, you'll convince them to adopt your faith. If you get them to fall for you, the theory goes, then you can sweet-talk them into falling for Jesus. Classic bait and switch.

Now, I'm not trying to police your love life here, but let's look at the logic of that, or rather the lack of logic. First, you have no control over someone else's faith and belief system. You can be the perfect example of Christian love and charity and not see any change whatsoever because God created all of us with this little thing called free will.

Second, you're potentially setting yourself up for a lot of pain. If it doesn't work, then what? Will you break up? Marry them and keep trying? There are a lot of potential downsides here.

Third, you're undermining the best possible source of intimacy, which is shared faith. Connecting on a spiritual level is far more powerful than any other point of connection. Why deprive yourself of that intimacy?

Fourth, you aren't being fair to the other person. You are conditioning your acceptance of them on their faith decision, which puts them in a tough place. Does that sound like something love would do?

Finally, don't you think they might be doing the same thing to you? That is, trying to convert you to their way of thinking, their value system, their priorities? In other words, they're going a different direction and hoping you'll join them. The prophet Amos wrote, "Can two people walk together without agreeing on the direction?" (Amos 3:3 NLT). The apostle Paul put it even more bluntly, "Do not be yoked together with unbelievers" (2 Corinthians 6:14). You can't walk in the same direction if you disagree on who you're following.

Be Honest

Nothing ruins a relationship like broken trust, and nothing breaks trust like dishonesty. Be honest with two people: yourself and the person you're dating. I'm not sure which of the two is easier to deceive, but I suspect the former.

Be honest with yourself about your motives. Are you in this for a bit of quick fun, with no intention of getting serious? Are you just lonely? Is this a social game? Does being wanted by someone stroke your ego? Are you bored? Is it force of habit or peer pressure? Or do you really love and care for the person? Dehydrated dating is all about meeting *your* needs, but true love is about caring for someone *else's* needs.

Be honest with each other about your idiosyncrasies and weaknesses. I'm not saying you should be awkwardly transparent about your snoring problem on your first date, but if the goal is intimacy and security, you're going to have to lower your defenses sooner or later. You don't gain anything by pretending to be someone you're not. I understand wanting to make a good first impression and to be the best version of yourself, but don't be a fake version of yourself. You're worth more than that. Your value is not tied to your perfection—so don't stay with anyone who implies that it is. Be vulnerable, but be secure in your vulnerability, and watch how the person responds. It will say a lot about them. It might be all you need to know.

Deal with Conflict

If you're hoping to live under the same roof and share the same bed with another human being someday, get used to dealing with conflict. It's amazing what dumb little things can spark conflict between two people. If I told you the issues DawnCheré and I have had fights over, you'd either laugh or ask for a refund on this book. Humans get mad. Tired. Hurt. Hungry. Ticked off. You can't avoid that, but you can learn how to deal with it. You have a few options here.

> Sweep it under the rug.
> Always be the martyr.
> Impose your will no matter what.
> Manipulate and shame them.
> Go into attack mode.
> Walk out and slam the door.
> Give them the silent treatment.
> Smile on the outside and die a little on the inside.
> Resolve it like mature adults.

You can probably guess which one I'd recommend. That's not the one I always follow when DawnCheré' and I argue, at least not at first—but it's my goal. And it's DawnCheré's goal as well. I can honestly say that our fights have brought us closer and moved us forward. Handling conflict is never easy, but the willingness to seek a resolution and fight for a relationship is absolutely essential.

You can learn a lot from someone by the way they fight.

I know these four things—going slow physically, not dating someone who isn't following Jesus, being honest, and resolving conflict—barely scratch the surface of the complexities of modern dating. I hope they help, but honestly, you don't need me to tell you how to live or date. You've got this. God is with you. You will know the way, and the person, and the timing as you walk this out. The journey to find love isn't always easy, but it is *your* journey, and you'll remember it for the rest of your life.

***

If you are getting married in a week, you can be as thirsty as you want. At that point, passionate desire is to be expected. Of course, if you were days away from your wedding, you probably wouldn't be reading a book for singles, so I guess it's a moot point. But assuming you're single and still in the hunt, it's time to ditch dehydrated dating and to quit dating thirsty people. Thirty and flirty is one thing—thirty and thirsty is another. By now, I'm sure you can tell the difference, regardless of your age.

You don't have to be thirsty. And you don't have to be with someone who is. Be secure. Be complete. Be satisfied with who you are and who you're becoming, with who God has made you to be and what he is doing in your life. Then find someone who feels the same, start a conversation, and see what happens. Worst-case scenario, you go on a date or two and then naturally drift apart. More likely, you'll become at least friends. And maybe, just maybe, the friendship will lead to something more, and you'll find love to be closer, and easier, and more beautiful than you thought you could have imagined.

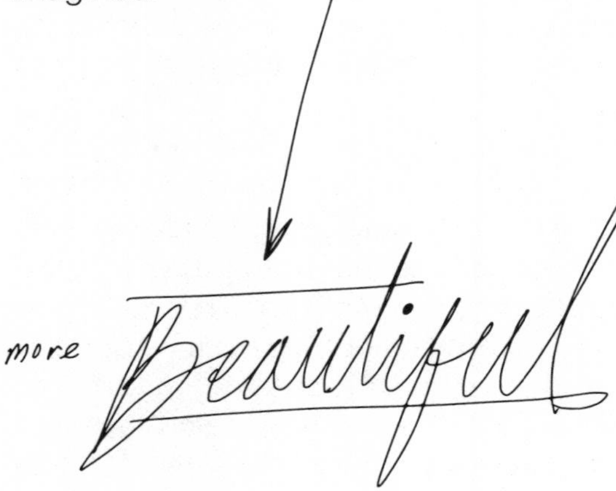

FABRICE'S STORY

It's all true. So often, we are so thirsty for love that we imagine that person will satisfy our soul. However, that's usually not the case, and we end up leaving the failed relationship more dehydrated, frustrated, and, in some instances, ashamed. That's because people don't satisfy our souls, Christ does. We know this, but... There's always a "but."

On average, the human body can survive without water for three days, weak, feeble, and on the brink of death. Imagine what our spirits feel when we haven't been in his Word for three days: weak, feeble, and... well, the spirit doesn't die, but it is silenced. So we go out there with a weak spirit overcompensating with our aggressive flesh. It's a recipe for disaster, as Pastor Rich says.

Throughout the years, I've learned there is one common denominator I must have in my singleness and relationships: being secure in Christ. I realized growing into adulthood that I was full of fear. Afraid to ask her out, afraid to commit, afraid to express how I really felt. I thought I was being rational and logical—you know, giving it time to cultivate, when in fact, I was just afraid of rejection and failure (sometimes before it even started).

It wasn't until I came to a place of confidence rooted solely in who Christ said I am and not who I thought was that I found the power to fear less. And eventually, in Christ Jesus, I became fearless. That's when the big picture slowly began to reveal itself. There is work to be done in my singleness that will guide the way to my purpose and ultimately into every relationship I have and will ever have. I decided I don't want to live in a desert full of mirages. I want to be so immersed in his presence and so hydrated that I'm able to overflow into all the relationships in my life. Being thirsty to date is exhausting; being thirsty for Christ, however, is where it's at.

10 LET'S TALK ABOUT SEX

SEX

WHEN I WAS A KID, MY SIBLINGS and I spent every Wednesday afternoon with my Aunt Marie, who was nearly eighty years old and lived in a retirement home. In retrospect, this weekly invasion by several preteens was probably more of a trial than a blessing for staff and residents. We had good intentions, though.

My aunt usually wanted us to do puzzles together. The only problem was, they were old puzzles and the original boxes had long since been lost, which meant there was no image to follow. I remember staring at random pieces in my hand and having no idea what they were or how they fit into the bigger picture—because I didn't even know what the bigger picture was.

A similar dynamic is often at work when it comes to the topics of sexuality, purity, and intimacy. Without a clear picture of what we're trying to build, it's hard to know what to do. We need context. We need vision. We need an understanding of the bigger picture.

As far as "fitting the pieces together," I'm pretty sure the mechanics of sex need no explanation. But the mechanics of sex are easy compared to understanding the dynamics of sex—its purposes, how it intersects with other facets of a relationship, and how to get the most from it. To have a healthy view of sex, we need context. We need to see how the sexual act fits into the bigger pictures of our lives, including our identity, our self-worth, our calling, and our goals.

It's a fun topic, even though it makes some people uncomfortable. So, hold on for the ride!

PURITY > VIRGINITY

This might be obvious to some (and scandalous to others), but virginity is not God's highest priority in your life. He does not have a giant ledger in the sky with every person listed in two columns: virgin or non-virgin. If someone does sleep with someone else, he doesn't clench his teeth, roll his eyes, groan thunderously, and move their name from one column to the other.

We know that. But biblical teachings that are meant to encourage sexual purity have often been used to portray God as the sex police. Principles that should bring freedom can instead create shame, guilt, and hurt.

I don't want to do that here.

If you are not a virgin now, or if you compromises your moral standards before marriage in some way, your value does not change. God's love for you does not go away. Your right standing and acceptance before him remains the same. Settle that in your mind and heart now, because shame and self-condemnation never did anyone any good.

The Bible's teachings about sex are not meant to idolize virginity or heap guilt on people who have had sex outside marriage. They are intended to show the value of sexual purity and help you live as freely as possible from the pain that wrong choices can bring. That's it.

"Purity" means freedom from contamination or sin. Pure water, for example, is water you can drink because it doesn't have contaminants in it. Likewise, sexual purity means sexuality that is free from contaminants or things that would damage or dilute it. It means guarding your sexuality for you and your future spouse, not out of fear, but out of honor and respect for the wholeness, value, and beauty of that relationship.

It's important to remember that sexual purity is not about what you did in the past but what you're allowing in the present. Even if you made unhealthy choices in the past, you can choose purity today. It's a state of mind, not a state of perfection; a walk you're on each day, not a finish line you reach or a test you already failed.

I think the shame attached to sexual purity comes when people make the issue of sex entirely about avoiding failure.

Some approaches to purity seem to focus mostly on what you did wrong rather than on what you are doing right. On how far you went that one time, how you compromised with that person, and how that's going to come back to haunt you on your wedding night.

Some of us grew up with well-meaning youth pastors who illustrated sexual purity by passing a bouquet of flowers down a row of young people, telling each kid to damage the bouquet more and more. As person after person ripped out flowers and leaves, the room would fall silent. The mutilated state of the flowers by the time they reached the end of the row was supposed to illustrate a young person who gave themselves away sexually to multiple people, and how their sexuality and eventual marriage would be irrevocably harmed. It was well intentioned but also terrifying. And more damaging, and theologically wrong, than we realized at the time.

It's true that any relationship that involves intimacy (whether sexual or emotional) opens you up to being hurt because breakups are so painful. Your life may bear scars from some of those relationships. But that doesn't mean your life is forever left in shreds if you've made some wrong choices.

God certainly doesn't see you that way. That's where the bouquet metaphor goes wrong for me because God's mercies are new every morning. Even if you've run far from him, even if your life has been anything but pure, forgiveness and grace continually cover you. Don't let the mistakes of your past convince you that sexual purity is out of reach. Purity is a choice each day, in each situation, with each relationship.

The point of sexual purity is not virginity or abstinence for their own sake: the goal is love, health, peace, and freedom. Virginity won't get you into heaven and immorality won't send you to hell. But the presence or absence of purity can definitely affect your life here on Earth. Why? Because sex has a uniquely powerful ability to cause great pleasure or great pain, to heighten intimacy or to undermine it, to build trust or to destroy it.

The goal of learning about God's purpose for your sexuality, therefore, is not to harm, hinder, or hurt you, but to help you. Purity, as the Bible teaches it, is not meant to restrict but to liberate. It sets you free.

Free from wrong views of sexuality and self-worth.
Free from addictions.
Free from regret and painful memories.
Free from constant lust.
Free from distractions.
Free from hurting other people sexually.
Free to rule your body.
Free to decide your priorities.
Free to walk in love toward others.
Free to celebrate your body, not worship it.
Free to enjoy your body and your sexuality.
Free to have the best sex, in the right context.
Free to move on if you make mistakes.
Free to choose what is best for you.

Contrary to popular opinion, the Bible does not look down on sex or imply that sex is wrong. From the moment of creation onward, when Adam and Eve were naked together without shame, we find a positive view of sexuality in the Bible. That positive view, though, is based on keeping sex in the right context, which is seeing it for what it is (and for what it isn't) within the larger picture of who you are meant to be.

A healthy view of sex means you value sex without worshiping it. You can look forward to it without being obsessed with it. You can choose how to use your time, energy, imagination, emotions, and body because God has given you a brain to understand what is best for you, to keep your feelings under your control, and to make good choices.

I get tired of people dismissing "God's view of sex" as negative or harmful when they don't even know what God's view is. People do this to God all the time, and not just on the topic of sex. "God says this." "God meant that." "God condemns this." "God prohibits that." Meanwhile, God must be thinking, *Bro, you made that up. I didn't say any of that.*

It's not always the fault of those people. Often, harmful views of sex have been subtly, or not so subtly, promoted by well-meaning Christian authors, blog writers, pastors, and parents. If you've been hurt by teachings or doctrines that promote shame, guilt, fear, or legalism in the name of God, I'm sorry. However, the answer isn't to turn from God or reject the Bible's teachings about sexuality. The answer is to replace such harmful beliefs with healthy ones. It's to see the big picture, the vision God has for your life, and to figure out where your sexuality fits into that.

If someone is going to reject God's view of sex, that's their choice—but they should at least understand it first. He's on our side, after all, and he's the one who invented sex in the first place. He knows how it's supposed to work. To better understand the biblical context for sex—the big picture—let's look at how and why sex started in the first place.

THE INVENTION OF SEX

Sex and marriage make their appearance very early in the Bible. The first chapter in the first book of the Bible describes the creation of humanity this way: "Then God said, 'Let us make mankind in our image, in our likeness. . . .' So God created mankind in his own image, in the image of God he created them; male and female he created them" (Genesis 1:26, 28).

Before we continue, did you catch the pronoun use there? "Let *us* make mankind in *our* image, in *our* likeness." Does God have multiple personalities? Is he talking to himself up there? No. Many Bible interpreters believe that this is the earliest indication of the Trinity: God as Father, Son, and Holy Spirit. He is three persons in one God, but he is still one God, not three gods. It's a concept that is difficult—maybe impossible—for the human brain to fully comprehend. However, the creation of man and woman and their unity in marriage is a beautiful reflection of the Trinity. Their union actually helps us understand the Trinity a little better.

The creation story continues in Genesis 2. I won't quote it here, but you can read it if you need a refresher. First, God created Adam from the dust of the ground. Then he stated that it was not good for the man to be alone. So, from one of Adam's ribs, God created Eve.

What was God saying about himself when he created Eve as a companion for Adam? That his image was not fully represented by a male human being. Even though the Bible uses masculine pronouns for God, God is bigger than either sex. Male and female *together* represent his image, but neither can fully represent him apart from the other.

I'm not saying you can't reflect God if you're single—don't get me wrong. What I am saying is that the creation of human beings as male and female was not meant to divide us or to place one sex above another, but rather to point back to the fullness of God. Both sexes constitute a beautiful symbol of the diversity and unity of God.

After creating Eve, the narrative states, "That is why a man leaves his father and mother and is united to his wife, and they become one flesh" Genesis 2:24). In other words, two people come together and essentially become a third person, a new person, one flesh. Can you see the parallel to the Trinity here?

Much as God is three in one, Adam and Eve were now two in one. They were separate but not separable; they were distinct but not divisible. We could take it even further and say that—in a spiritual sense—a couple united in God is actually *three* in one

God is three

Much as God is three in one, Adam and Eve were now two in one. They were separate but not separable; they were distinct but not divisible.

because God is in the midst of them.

I don't mean to sound too mystical or esoteric here, but the Bible is full of symbolism, and symbols matter. When the Bible describes a couple as becoming one flesh, it presents the marriage covenant as a representation of God's very image. Two people coming together as one is a direct reflection of the nature of God.

So, how does this apply to sex? Sex, biblically speaking, was created within the context of the marriage covenant. It is a sign and symbol of this covenant in all its intimacy, purity, and promise. Sex is also a privilege of the covenant, reserved for those two people (and only those two people) to enjoy together, freely and without shame. It is a passionate expression of the oneness of two individuals made in the image of God, two individuals whose intimacy reflects the nature of God in a way they could not on their own.

That means that sex, in a very real sense, is spiritual.

They probably didn't tell you that in biology class. It's true, though. Sex is not just physical, or emotional, or hormonal. It's not merely some animal instinct. It has a profoundly spiritual component that helps unite two people as one. Sex is not just a physical act but also a spiritual one.

> That's why sex in the right context can heal so much.
> That's why sex out of context can hurt so much.
> That's why sex unites two people so closely, so quickly.
> That's why sex is so often on our minds and so natural for our bodies.
> That's why sex inspires so many songs, poems, and vows.
> That's why we want it so much.
> That's why we expect so much out of it.

Because it's not just a physical thing; it's a point of soul-level intimacy between two people. And that's why it's so important to understand it and to guard it.

I'm not being legalistic or puritanical, and you don't have to agree with me. But I believe God designed sex to function best within marriage because it is an essential part of the oneness a couple experiences. It's the physical joining of two people's bodies who are also joined spiritually into one flesh.

We don't worship sex. That's not what I mean by it being spiritual. This is the bigger picture you need to see when you're trying to assemble the puzzle pieces of your sexuality, your desires, your need for intimacy, your romantic attraction, and your hormones. You need to see a picture of oneness with another person on all levels, spiritual, emotional, and physical. A picture of being made in the image of God, all over again, not as one person now, but as two.

SEX WITH A PURPOSE

It's essential to understand that sex came into existence within the context of the marriage bond because the creation of anything points to its purpose. The socks you are wearing were made to keep your feet warm and dry. The chair or couch on which you're seated was designed so you wouldn't have to crouch on the floor. Caller ID was invented so you could ignore incoming calls from people you are avoiding. So, to get a better picture of the place sex should occupy in your life, let's look at the three primary purposes of sex that we see in Scripture.

Procreation

One of the primary purposes of sex is procreation. Duh, right? I've known that since second grade when I asked my mom where babies came from and she told me to ask my dad. You might be tempted to skip this one—first, because it's so obvious, and second because having children might be far off in your future—but keep reading. I want to say some things you probably didn't hear from your dad or your sex ed teacher.

Here's the big idea: *marriage and sex reflect God's creative nature.* We participate in the creative power of God through the family.

It didn't have to work this way. God could have created Adam and Eve, then twenty years later cooked up another batch of humans and dropped them onto the planet, then twenty years later another, and so on.

But he didn't.

He shared not only life with us, but also the ability to produce life. He didn't just create us, he gave us creative capacity. Growth, expansion, and creativity are aspects of God's nature, and so they are aspects of human beings created in his image.

That is not a small thing. It is an incredible, profound reality.

We are not just bringing children into the world. We are not just populating the planet. We are not just following some instinct, like the birds and the bees and the flowers and the trees. No, we are bringing God's greatest masterpiece into existence on this planet.

Humans are God's highest creation, the pinnacle of his work. We are the only beings made in God's image. Mountain ranges aren't made in God's image. Neither are the moon and stars, the beach and the ocean, the fish and animals. Only humans carry this privilege. Paul calls us "God's handiwork" (Ephesians 2:10). We are his finest work, and we are infinitely valuable to him.

Every human is. Every baby is. And sex is the gift through which we literally create more humans. That should scare you a little and excite you a lot, all at the same time.

Pleasure

The fact that sex is for procreation is obvious, and so is the fact that it is for *pleasure.* Listening to some Christians talk, though,

Humans are God's highest creation, the pinnacle of his work. We are the only beings made in God's image... We are his finest work, and we are infinitely valuable to him.

you might get the impression that they think God created sex solely to make babies, and then the devil threw in the whole pleasure thing when God wasn't looking, just so we'd mess things up by falling into sin.

God did not have to make sex so fun. Much of the animal world reproduces in very unsexy ways. God could have created us to lay eggs, for example. He didn't have to make sex so pleasurable that you probably think about it nearly every day, if not multiple times a day.

Stop feeling guilty about that. I'm not saying you should act on those thoughts in an immoral way, of course, or that sex should fill your mind all the time. I'm just saying that the pleasure of sex is a good thing. Enjoying sex is a holy thing. It's not just the reproductive aspect of it that glorifies God; it's the enjoyment of something he created for our good and our pleasure.

There is an entire book of the Bible the celebrates the joys of romance and sex. It's a love poem called Song of Solomon. This ancient little book doesn't just reference sexual pleasure in passing, as if it were a necessary evil or a fact of life to be glossed over. Not at all. It gives graphic, explicit, NSFW details of exactly what two people wanted to do to each other in bed. Many of those details are cloaked in poetry and metaphor, but if you take the time to understand their meaning, you'll find yourself blushing, cheering, aroused, or all of the above.

According to God's Word, sex in marriage is freeing. It is fun. It is pleasurable. It is to be enjoyed. It should be exciting. It should turn you on. It should get all of the right things happening in your body and in your fantasies.

The same person who wrote Song of Solomon, (King Solomon, of course) wrote most of the book of Proverbs, including this:

> Drink water from your own cistern,
> running water from your own well.

> Should your springs overflow in the streets,
> your streams of water in the public squares?
> Let them be yours alone,
> never to be shared with strangers.
> May your fountain be blessed,
> and may you rejoice in the wife of your youth.
> A loving doe, a graceful deer—
> may her breasts satisfy you always,
> may you ever be intoxicated with her love.
> (Proverbs 5:15-19)

Again with the metaphors. You can probably figure out what Solomon meant by "drinking from your own cistern" and not letting your "springs overflow in the streets." It was his way of saying, "Keep it in your pants."

He doesn't stop there, though. Sexual purity in marriage is not about exercising iron resolve to never cheat on your spouse. It's about enjoying your spouse and having fulfilling sex throughout your life.

That line, "May her breasts satisfy you always, may you ever be intoxicated with her love," is not some wish or a toast at the wedding. It's a literal choice you make. It's a goal you set. It's a reality you make happen by deciding to value and celebrate your spouse above everyone else and to the exclusion of everyone else.

Think about the words:

> *May* = let this happen, strive for this to happen, make it true
> *Her* = just hers or his, and nobody else's
> *Breasts* = the body of your spouse, especially the sexual parts
> *Satisfy* = fully enrapture and fulfill
> *You* = not somebody else—just you, and always you
> *Always* = until death do you part

He's speaking to men in this particular passage, but the truths apply to everyone, as Song of Solomon shows. Husbands and wives were created to enjoy one another's bodies and the intimacy and pleasure of sex throughout their marriage.

There is no sex like married sex. Like Song of Solomon sex. Like Proverbs 5 sex. It is exciting, thrilling, and satisfying.

So many people have the wrong idea of sex in marriage. They think illicit sex is the best sex. That one-night stands are the best sex. That a couple of dates and a night of drinking and ending up in bed with someone you barely know is somehow romantic. That sex without commitment or expectations is more fulfilling than the trust and intimacy that a marriage covenant provides.

I'm not claiming that sex outside of marriage will be terrible and you'll hate it. I'm sure it feels good in the moment. What I'm saying, though, is that you need to raise your expectations for sex *within* marriage. Sex can be everything you dreamed and hoped it to be, and even more.

For one thing, sex within marriage gets better with time because you get better with practice. You find new ways to pleasure each other. You learn the likes and dislikes of the other. You experiment together, laugh together, explore together, have fun together. You build trust. You create history. You grow in confidence. Sex is a dance, and the more you dance with the same person, the more you think and move as one.

Married sex, in my opinion, is the best sex because it is supported by trust, commitment, transparency, consistency, and experience. That's not to say it's awesome every time. Sometimes you'll be tired, or stressed, or distracted. That's fine. Let's not make sex so high pressure. Sex is not meant to be a one-time experience but rather an ongoing part of your relationship. And overall, from the perspective of time, a healthy sex life with a committed partner will be more satisfying than illicit affairs or one-night stands could ever be.

Of course, your marriage has to be healthy to enjoy sex

because sex depends on trust and intimacy. Good sex can't fix a bad relationship, no matter what you've seen in the movies. Sooner or later, you have to stop touching and start talking. So if you are married and sex isn't what it used to be or should be, figure out why. Get some counseling if you need to—there's no shame in that. There are likely some underlying issues that are affecting more than just your sex life, and if the two of you can work through those, you'll be healthier all around.

The pleasure of sex is one of God's greatest gifts in a marriage, and it only gets better with time.

Protection

Procreation and pleasure are the two most obvious reasons for sex, but there's a third reason as well. A healthy sexual relationship provides *protection* for a couple. I'm not talking about condoms. That's a different kind of protection. I'm talking about the emotional and relational bond created by sex, a bond that helps insulate a couple against affairs or other harmful sexual activity outside of the relationship.

Speaking of sexual relations, the apostle Paul wrote, "Do not deprive each other except perhaps by mutual consent and for a time, so that you may devote yourselves to prayer. Then come together again so that Satan will not tempt you because of your lack of self-control" (1 Corinthians 7:5).

In other words, if you're not having sex, you're praying. Not every minute of every day—that would be exhausting (whether prayer or sex). Paul is saying that, as a married couple, unless you've decided to take an agreed-upon time apart to seek God, your sex life should be active. In other words, you shouldn't withhold sex, or neglect sex, or get too busy for sex, or use sex as a bargaining chip, or manipulate your partner with sex. Why? Because it is a gift to enjoy as a couple, and it should be a regular, beautiful part of your marriage, with no strings attached.

Lack of sex in a marriage, Paul says, can contribute to one

When God talks about morality and purity, he's not trying to limit you. He's trying to serve you. He's giving you a picture of what sex was made for and how it can benefit you.

or both of you giving in to temptation. That's what he means by Satan tempting the couple because of their lack of self-control.

Before I continue, I know that some might read that and say to their spouse, "Hey, did you read 1 Corinthians 7? It's your job to protect me from temptation with regular sex, and it's your fault if I fall." That's ridiculous. They are using Scripture to get what they want or to blame their partner for their own failings. That is absolutely not what Paul is saying nor what I am implying here. If you choose to act on sexual urges outside the bonds and bounds of marriage, that's on you.

Having said that, though, we can make it easier on ourselves and each other by having a healthy sex life. We aren't slaves to our impulses, but those impulses are real, and they are strong, and they were meant to be satisfied. So satisfy them within marriage. That's all Paul is saying here. He is reminding us that sex doesn't just feel good and make babies; it also protects the couple.

Have you ever seen commercials for sugar-loaded breakfast cereals? Usually, the cereal in question appears on a table surrounded by fruit, eggs, toast, orange juice, and milk. At the end of the commercial, a small text box appears on the screen: "Sugar Bombs, a delicious part of your nutritious breakfast." In other words, the cereal is tasty but useless. Some people see sex like that: it's the delicious part of marriage. The fun part. Not essential, and maybe even distracting, but enjoyable and fun.

I disagree. Strongly. Not with the fun part, but with the "it's-delicious-but-has-zero-actual-value" part. Sex is far more critical to marriage than cereal is to breakfast. That's the understatement of the year. It's delicious, for sure, but it also builds a marriage. It feeds a marriage. Sex should be its own food group, in this metaphor, toward the top of that food pyramid thing. Okay, that might be pushing it a little, but you get my point: sex strengthens a marriage.

This is vital because we are bombarded with messaging

that twists God's purposes for sex and marriage. These cultural values downplay the value or enjoyment of sex within marriage and exaggerate the pleasures of sex outside of it. There is no harm, they say, in experimenting sexually, having an affair, going to strip clubs, trying a threesome, or any other number of things that will ultimately take from your relationship, not add to it. Healthy romance and sexual intimacy protect a marriage by keeping you focused on enjoying one another, instead of losing sight of what you care most about in pursuit of a passing pleasure you'll probably regret for years to come.

Good sex is both a *sign* of a healthy marriage and a *key* to a healthy marriage. That is, it shows that other aspects of the relationship are working, and it enhances those other aspects, as well. What aspects? Trust, respect, communication, emotional bonding, time together, friendship, mutual dependency, shared experiences, serving one another, romance, intimacy, joy, gratitude, admiration, and marital satisfaction—to name a few. Sex can't restore those things if they're missing, but it can help build them, and it can help keep them from being lost in the first place.

When God talks about morality and purity, he's not trying to limit you. He's trying to serve you. He's giving you a picture of what sex was made for and how it can benefit you. From *procreation* to *pleasure* to *protection*, God meant for sex to be a blessing and a gift.

SEX MYTHS

Those three purposes are easy enough to understand and accept on a general level, but to be honest, sexuality is more complicated and nuanced than that. That's why there is so much confusion and misunderstanding around this topic—and often, so much pain. It's one thing to say sex is meant for procreation, pleasure, and protection, but it's another to know how to navigate the intricacy of intimacy in a specific romantic relationship—*yours*. That's when theory has to turn into practice.

This practical outworking of purity and wisdom is where people often find themselves struggling. They are surrounded by so many voices, so many opinions, so many options, so many decisions that they can't decide what is healthy and what is not. Often, they have believed myths about sexuality that are not doing them any favors. These myths gloss over the *benefits* of doing things the way God tells and the *pain* that comes from ignoring his commands. This isn't about religious prudishness, as I've said before, but about avoiding hurt and maximizing the joys of human sexuality.

In my conversations with singles and married couples over the years, there are several myths about sex that tend to come up frequently. Take a look at the following points and see if any of them have influenced your perspective about sex and purity. It might be time to reevaluate some perspectives or assumptions that are holding you back.

Myth 1: Sex Is Only Physical

Sex is *not* purely physical because humans can't compartmentalize things that way. Sex is holistic. It includes your body, yes, but also your emotions, your thoughts, and your soul. Sex is spiritual, as we discussed above. To limit it to the physical realm is to rob it of its deepest intimacy.

If sex were only physical, it wouldn't have such intense emotional effects on us. It wouldn't hold such a deep attraction for us. There wouldn't be so many regrets tied to unhealthy sexual encounters or so much pain caused by sexual abuse.

I'm not denying the physical appeal of sex, but the connection it creates cannot be isolated to the physical realm. To say sex is only physical is to deny the full effect (for good and for bad) that it has on two people.

Myth 2: I Need to Be an Experienced Lover to Enjoy My Wedding Night

The theory here is that by messing around sexually now, you'll be a better lover for your future spouse. The truth is, you don't get to be a good lover by being with a lot of different people. You get to be a good lover two ways: by *being with the same person a long time* and by *becoming a good person outside of the bedroom.* Being a good lover goes far beyond just knowing how to make someone feel good in bed.

Being with the same person matters because you get better with practice as you learn to move and feel as one. You can't even be a "good lover" on your own, if you think about it, because sex takes two people, and both people matter in the encounter. That means sex is less about being a good lover and more about being good lovers. Plural. Together. As one.

Becoming a good person means that who you are during the day matters more than who you are at night. It means learning to genuinely care about the feelings and experiences of the other person, not just yourself. You can have all the experience in the world, but if you're a selfish lover, you won't be a good lover.

Don't fall for the lie that you have to be with a lot of people so you can be ready to make the right one happy when the time comes. You'll figure it out. And you'll figure it out together, which is half the fun. Sure, the wedding night might be a little awkward. Who cares? There's no rush. You have your entire honeymoon and the rest of your life to figure this out.

The first night with anyone could be awkward, anyway, no matter how experienced you are. And what about the morning *after* a night like that? Even if the sex was good, is there anything more awkward than the infamous walk of shame after a one-night stand or an evening of drinking that went too far? It seems to me that a mildly awkward but beautiful wedding night, followed by a shame-free sexy morning, followed by a lifetime of beautiful moments shared with the same person beats anything. Choose your awkward, I guess.

Myth 3: Everybody Is Doing It

"Everybody is sleeping together. Everybody is living together. Everybody is hooking up." So goes the myth. But it's not true. They just talk about it when they do it, and they don't talk about it when they don't. That's human nature. Even if, say, 50 percent or 75 percent were doing it, that's still not everybody. They certainly aren't doing it all the time, either.

It almost goes without saying that just because a lot of people are doing something doesn't make it right. A lot of people can be wrong. You can probably think of a dozen examples from history where the majority was wrong. You don't have to do what "everybody" says. You are free to choose a different way.

Myth 4: Pornography Is Harmless

Pornography acts like a drug, and it might turn out to be one of the most destructive addictions of our generation. I can't tell you the number of people who have told me they hate it, but they can't seem to stop. They live with shame. They objectify people instead of caring about people. They can't find sexual pleasure or even reach climax during actual sex. They are consumed with sexual thoughts throughout the day. They are distracted, depressed, and tormented by feelings they are powerless to control.

I'm not projecting any of those things on you if you look at porn. Nor will I try to define what constitutes porn or what you should or shouldn't be looking at. That's not my role. It's something you should take seriously, though, because (as with any addiction) you can be your own worst enemy when it comes to denying there is a problem and justifying your behavior.

Porn teaches your mind and body three things, according to author and pastor Andy Stanley.[16] First, a *real body* isn't good enough. Second, *one body* isn't good enough. And third, *your spouse's body* isn't good enough. Maybe it turns you on for a bit, maybe it helps you relax temporarily, maybe it adds spice to your love life, but ultimately it takes far more than it gives.

Myth 5: It's Good to Try Before You Buy

This myth asks the hypothetical question, "What if I marry someone and find out we aren't compatible in bed?" What does that even mean? It's not like you have some ideal sex partner out there and no one else can satisfy you. You aren't buying a used car that needs to be test driven before you commit. Trust me, if you love each other, you're going to figure out how to have good sex together.

If it turns out you are "incompatible," it's not going to be because something didn't work in bed, but because something didn't work in some other aspect of the marriage. Turning the relationship into a sexual one will actually get in the way of discovering that kind of incompatibility. Learn to love each other without sex now, and sex will take care of itself later.

Myth 6: Broken Now Means Broken Forever

This myth states that if you've crossed a line sexually, there are no second chances. You messed up, you ruined your future marriage, you failed your spouse, you angered God, and you might as well give up on marital happiness.

If it turns out you are "incompatible," it's not going to be because something didn't work in bed, but because something didn't work in some other aspect of the

Hopefully, you can see through this one easily. This myth stems, at least in part, from the misguided views of virginity and purity that we talked about earlier. Don't confuse your value with your virginity. Don't base your future happiness on how well you performed in the past. That's not how God thinks, and it's not how grace works.

You are not broken; you are whole in Jesus. And the future is not written yet.

Myth 7: Monogamy Doesn't Work

You might have heard the claim that 50 percent of marriages end in divorce, and therefore marriage and monogamy are a failed social experiment. Why get married if you only have a one in two chance of making it?

First of all, even that stat tells us that a lot of marriages *do* work. At least half. Actually, if you do a little research, you discover the stat itself is wrong, and the question is a lot more nuanced. The 50 percent number is based on a simplistic (and erroneous) calculation that compares the number of marriages and divorces each year, rather than looking at the lifespan of actual marriages. Exact stats are impossible to calculate for various reasons, but professional estimates put the number of US marriages that end in divorce at closer to 45 percent, and that number is getting lower with each generation. Some researchers predict that within a few years, it could be around 33 percent.[17] In other words, more marriages succeed than fail.

Marriage is not doomed and monogamy is not fundamentally flawed. They are what you make them. Marriage works if you work it. You can't control all the variables of life, but if you're willing to learn, grow, and fight for your marriage—and if your partner is too, of course—then the odds are in your favor.

***

For a book written for singles, that was a lot of sex talk. I hope my comments help give you the big picture of the puzzle you're trying to put together. At the end of the day, only you can decide how to live. Only you can know what purity looks like for you.

Sexuality is a beautiful thing. It's God's gift to you, and the last thing he wants is for you to live in shame, guilt, or fear. Instead, be confident in who you are now, and decide to enjoy the journey. Take some of the pressure off. Give yourself room to feel, to fall in love, to make mistakes, to learn, to grow.

It's not easy to navigate relationships, purity, romance, and intimacy. You probably won't do it all exactly right.

That's okay.

God is with you, and his grace and mercy are enough for you. As you live in love, as you grow in grace, as you walk in wisdom, you'll find your way. And you'll have a lot of fun doing it.

GREG'S STORY

As a teen, I was exposed to pornography, but I kept it a secret. My little secret. I knew it was bad, but I felt that if I could hide it from people, I could hide it from God. No harm, no foul. I still served in church and was a mentor to other kids and a leader in my community, but all the while, I was keeping my little secret to myself.

Eventually, as an adult, I entered a few serious relationships, and my private sexual life started to become more public. I couldn't help myself. I had trained my body and my mind to want certain things. I engaged in activities I knew I wasn't supposed to. I compromised my integrity and what I had always stood for just so I could satisfy my physical desires. I had trained my brain to be selfish, to get what I wanted when I wanted it, and to not care about who I hurt in the process. I didn't know it, but the person I was hurting the most was myself.

I was searching for love, but I was settling for lust.

I thought getting married would solve my problems. I thought a marriage bond would be enough to fight the temptation to look at porn or think impure thoughts about others. I was wrong. It only got worse. Marriage seemed to only magnify my problems.

But it wasn't just a sexual addiction, it was an entire way of thinking. I had become selfish, insecure, self-seeking. The world revolved around me. Everyone else was wrong; I was right. At least that's how my actions played out. I was snappy and irritable. Nothing like the person of Jesus. I thought hiding my sin meant I could control it. But it wasn't until I learned to give my whole life to God, even my darkest secrets, that I found freedom. But that didn't come easy.

My marriage was ending, and for more than one reason. There were a hundred different things I wish I had done dif-

ferently. Staying pure was one of them. I thought I could turn it around. But my credibility was lost. I had compromised my integrity. I traded the man I always wanted to be for the temporary satisfaction I was used to. Something which started so small and seemed to be insignificant had ruined my relationships and now my life.

I needed a change. I poured my heart out to a few close friends and my leaders at VOUS. I started to serve with every free moment I had. I gave my hands no idle time. I had to rewire my brain with new habits, new routines, new boundaries.

I had to die to the old self and put on the new. I dove into Scripture and begged the Lord to help me through it.

And you know what? God surrounded me with a community of strength. People who didn't condemn me for my sins but who encouraged me. I felt as if God humbled me to my very core and started to build me up again on a new foundation.

As I began to heal, I made non-negotiables for myself. Things I wouldn't compromise on, no matter how much I wanted to please people or myself. I knew God would reward my obedience. I had tried my own way and failed miserably, and now it was time to do it God's way.

I took a stand. No more porn. No more premarital sex. No lying. No hiding.

I wanted to be clean in the eyes of man and the eyes of God.

And can I tell you? God's grace knows no bounds. Today, I'm happily married to my soulmate. There's truth, honesty, forgiveness, and grace. God met me halfway and then some. His strength was truly found in my weakness. All I had to do was let go and believe that God wants what's best for me.

Best for Me.

11 CRITICAL RELA-TIONSHIP QUES-TIONS

I WAS SEVENTEEN WHEN DAWNCHERÉ and I met, and we were twenty-two and twenty-one when we were married. That's young, I know. When we tell people that, they look at us suspiciously, as if we must have had either a shotgun wedding or an arranged marriage. Neither was the case. We just made up our minds early on. Plus, I wasn't dumb—I knew if I didn't move fast, some other dude might swoop in and try to steal her away.

For me, it was love at first sight. For DawnCheré, it was love after a couple of fights. Over fifteen years later, we're still together and still in love. So I'd say it worked out well for us.

We don't have a perfect marriage (does anyone?). But we decided a long time ago we wanted to continually improve our relationship. We're willing to invest in it because it matters to us. If that means work, we'll work. If it means humility, we'll be humble. If it means asking for advice from people who have been on this road longer than we have, we'll get advice.

Over the years, we've realized something: we didn't know each other or love each other like we thought we did when we got married. We've found out a lot of things along the way. We've had to ask ourselves some hard questions and deal with some issues within our own hearts in order to guard our intimacy and keep the promises we made to each other so many years ago.

That's normal. Relationships take work. I don't think the work aspect of romantic attachments gets enough airtime, though. We'd rather think that romance and butterflies override our humanity and turn us into fourth and fifth members of the Trinity. That a ring on our finger means our inner demons are banished forever.

Author and philosopher Alain de Botton wrote a darkly humorous essay for the *New York Times* titled, "Why You Will Marry the Wrong Person." His premise was that we are all flawed, and therefore there is no perfect mate out there for anyone. That is, no human could possibly fix all our problems and be everything we need.

Not only that, he says, but we really can't know someone

(or even ourselves) until we grow close, and closeness takes time. That means that even after marriage, there will be a few surprises along the way. "We seem normal only to those who don't know us very well," he writes. "In a wiser, more self-aware society than our own, a standard question on any early dinner date would be: 'And how are you crazy?'"[18]

There's a lot of truth in that. It would make for more interesting conversations than the weather or the quality of the steak you're eating.

"Nobody's perfect," de Botton continues. "The problem is that before marriage, we rarely delve into our complexities.... One of the privileges of being on our own is therefore the sincere impression that we are really quite easy to live with."

Ouch.

His conclusion? That we need to stop idolizing the Western, romanticized view of love that elevates feelings above all else. Our overemphasis on goosebumps and warm fuzzies sets us up for failure when the other person lets us down or when romantic ecstasy has to share the stage with mundane reality. Instead, he argues, we should admit that all relationships have problems, and all people have weaknesses. Rather than being surprised by that, we can work with it.

There's a lot of truth to that, too.

Having a realistic view of a marriage relationship (or any relationship, for that matter) is a good thing. I'm not saying that you should allow the fact that "everybody has problems" to justify an abusive relationship, nor should it make you give up on improving. We'll talk more about that later. However, if you recognize that a healthy romantic relationship will take work, patience, and a good sense of humor, you'll be way better prepared for long-term love than most people are.

Short-term love is easy, by the way. It burns on emotion and superficiality. It is a beautiful thing, but it's only the kindling of love, quick-burning flames designed to grow into lifelong, covenant love.

Long-term love is fueled not just by feelings but by honesty. On authenticity. On vulnerability. On shared experiences, mutual trust, hours of late-night talks, dumb inside jokes, and a lot of forgiveness. This kind of relationship grows as two people become intimately acquainted with each other, as they get to know the good, the bad, the ugly, and still choose love.

How do you make this kind of long-term relationship work? Well, I can't tell you. Not absolutely, anyway. A relationship takes two people, two unique individuals, which means that the dynamics in any relationship are as diverse as the number of humans on the planet. That's what makes this thing called love so beautiful, intimate, and personal—you have to figure it out together.

Having said that, though, I have ten questions you can ask yourself frequently, both during the dating process and periodically throughout your marriage. These questions will help you assess your relationship in order to grow, change, and improve as needed. Some quick disclaimers, though.

- If you don't plan on getting married soon or ever, that's fine. You're single and secure. Skip this chapter or use it to help a friend.
- These questions are directed at you because you can't force change on someone else. But don't assume that a problematic relationship is always your fault. If needed, discuss the questions with your significant other as well.
- If you have genuine concerns about the person you're dating, be willing to put the relationship on pause or even to break up. That's the idea behind dating, isn't it?
- If you're already married, ignore the previous point (unless there are biblical grounds for separation or divorce). Instead, use these questions to improve your relationship going forward.

Relationships take wisdom and work—especially when you start to see just how crazy each of you are, as Alain da Button pointed out. There's nothing wrong with that. It's the path to real intimacy, and it's well worth the investment. As you grow in any romantic relationship, use the following questions to keep you focused on relationship health.

1. WHO COMPLETES YOU?

There is a misconception that often permeates the movies we watch, the books we read, the conversations we have about romance, and even the fanfare of weddings we attend: that the person you marry will somehow complete you. We looked at this myth—and the ridiculous weight it places on a relationship—in chapter 1.

Apart from putting way too much pressure on one poor human being, this belief underestimates and undervalues *you.* You don't need a relationship to complete you because you are 100 percent "you" all on your own. If you are single, you aren't waiting for someone to come along and make you fully human or fully you. Marriage isn't about two half-humans coming together to make one whole human; it's about two already-whole humans coming together and forming a third entity, something new, which Genesis 2 calls "one flesh."

This new oneness is not more complete than either individual was on his or her own, but rather it is complete in a new way. People don't complete you; they complement you. They don't fix you; they add to you. Yes, they make life better, but that doesn't mean your life was incomplete without them.

That is the reality of following Jesus. He's the only one who can complete you. He provides the fulfillment and affirmation and acceptance your soul longs for. When you understand that and

That is the reality of following Jesus. He's the only one who can complete you. He provides the fulfillment and affirmation and acceptance your soul longs for.

your soul

stop using relationships to complete you, relationships become more fulfilling.

If you feel emptiness, desperation, or loneliness, the first person you should turn to is Jesus. He's not the only person—it's helpful to have physical, visible humans around you, too, because sometimes you just need a hug. But hugs can't complete you. A boyfriend won't make you whole. A girlfriend can't give you healthy self-esteem. Having kids won't heal the trauma of the past.

For those things, you need the infinite and faithful God of the universe. There is a part of you and me that will remain unfulfilled without knowing the love of Jesus. He is the only one who can bring completion to our lives.

For example, Jesus said to his disciples, "I have told you this so that my joy may be in you and that your joy may be complete" (John 15:11). It is Jesus who completes your joy. Your spouse can bring you joy, but they can't complete your joy. They can't make you perfectly satisfied.

Similarly, the prophet Isaiah, speaking to God, said, "You will keep in perfect peace those whose minds are steadfast, because they trust in you" (Isaiah 26:3). Your spouse can bring you peace, but they can't give you perfect peace.

The apostle John wrote, "God is love, and all who live in love live in God, and God lives in them. And as we live in God, our love grows more perfect" (1 John 4:16-17 NLT). Your spouse can offer you love, but they can't give you perfect love, nor can their love be perfected in you.

Perfect joy, perfect peace, perfect love—I could go on, but you get the picture. Only God is perfect. No matter how incredible your significant other might be, they would make a terrible god. They would make a miserable source of inner healing, self-worth, or life satisfaction. If you expect them to fill the role of God in your life, you'll only end up frustrating you both. Human love complements you, but only divine love completes you.

2. ARE YOU FEELING LOVE OR CHOOSING LOVE?

This is a bit of a trick question because you shouldn't have to pick one or the other, at least not all the time. Ideally, your relationship includes a lot of good feelings mixed in with some moments of choosing love over feelings.

If you're continually struggling to get along, if you're forever having to forgive things or overlook problems, if you're always fighting and making up and then fighting again, maybe you should evaluate whether you want to spend the rest of your life together. Love isn't always easy, but it's not supposed to be hard, either. It's a gift from God, not a cross to bear. More on that to come.

Most of the time, we put too much weight on feelings and not enough on choice. True love includes feelings, but it goes beyond them. It includes your mind and your will as well as your emotions. And your bank account, if I could throw that in there.

Reducing love to a feeling makes it self-focused and fleeting. And yet, you hear this idea about love in romantic movies all the time: "You make *me* happy. You're the only one for *me*. *I* can't live without you. *I* need you."

Such statements imply that love is mostly about you; it's about how you feel and whether or not your needs are being met. They suggest that if you're in love, you'll have some magnetic, fatalistic, irresistible attraction to the other person all the time—maybe even against your better judgment or the advice of your friends. And if that doesn't happen, well, either your love must have died, or the other person must be failing you somehow because it's their responsibility to make you feel madly and happily in love.

Limiting the experience of love to how you feel is selfish. It's self-focused, self-absorbed, and self-defeating. Love can't make you feel happy all the time. Not even God can do that—especially if your focus is on yourself. If love is little else to you but butterflies and happy feelings, you're going to be let down a lot because butterflies tend to fly away without warning.

True love includes feelings, of course, but feelings are the natural byproduct of selfless love, not the selfish pursuit of love. True love is the opposite of self-absorption. Love doesn't look inward; it looks outward. It is consistently others-focused. Love means you choose to value, serve, care for, protect, and lift up the other person.

That's why it must be a choice. Reread 1 Corinthians 13, if you haven't lately, and notice the characteristics of love listed there. Love is patient, for example. Does anyone ever "feel" patient? I sure don't. Especially when I most need to be patient. Patience is a choice. It says love is not easily angered, that it keeps no record of wrong. That's definitely a choice because your feelings will push you to do the opposite. You'll feel offended, you'll feel angered, you'll feel slighted. That is when you need love the most.

Feelings come, feelings go, and feelings come again—but true love remains.

3. IS ANYTHING FROM THE PAST KEEPING YOU FROM MOVING FORWARD?

When DawnCheré and I got married, we brought baggage into our relationship. Literally. It was a luggage set my in-laws gave us for our wedding. For the first year of our marriage, we stored that luggage under our bed. We never thought about it except when we were going to travel somewhere; then we'd go to the bedroom, pull it out, and use it.

Something similar happens when two people begin a relationship. They often bring with them baggage from the past. Maybe it's trauma, maybe it's bitterness, maybe it's bad habits, maybe it's harmful ways of communicating, or some other learned behavior. Most of the time, it stays hidden and forgotten. But when a fight happens, or when the stress level hits a certain point, or when some random scenario triggers forgotten fears, they reach under the bed and drag out the baggage so they can put it to use.

Baggage can come from your previous relationships, or it can be a result of your current relationship. Baggage from before could be someone who cheated on you, an abusive childhood, or anything else that had a profound effect on you. It's not your partner's fault, but they end up taking some of the consequences. Baggage from a current relationship refers to bitterness that builds up due to failings or conflict between you.

You might not be aware that the past is haunting you—until your boyfriend doesn't text you back one night, and you immediately start imagining him cheating on you. Or your girlfriend merely suggests that you work on changing some area, and it sends you into a tailspin of insecurity. We talked about being healed from the past earlier, so I'm not going to repeat that. Just be aware that strong emotions or reactions don't always mean something is going wrong right now—they might mean something went wrong a long time ago and you haven't resolved it.

If you are in a committed relationship, this can be a really good time to be vulnerable. Share what you experienced and how it is affecting you. If it's a recent offense you haven't forgiven, talk it out. Find solutions together. You'll be working through differences for the rest of your lives, so you might as well start now.

4. ARE YOU SURPRISED WHEN YOU CAN'T CHANGE SOMEONE ELSE?

Too many people assume marriage is going to fix everything. All you need is two rings and some vows, they think, and bad habits will go away. Laziness will transform into a work ethic. A wandering eye will turn into faithfulness. Abuse will magically become love.

It doesn't work that way.

Marriage doesn't fix problems. If anything, marriage magnifies problems because suddenly you have the compounding effect of two broken people living under one roof.

Of course, you will help cover each other's weaknesses and faults. We talked about that earlier. But helping your spouse where they are weak is not the same thing as expecting them to change and not be weak anymore. The first is your choice, your sacrifice, your service. The second is imposing your ideal upon someone else's free will, which starts to feel a lot like conditional love.

You can't change anyone, especially your spouse. You need to settle that in your heart and head now. You are only able to change yourself—and even that is a little iffy sometimes. It's not fair to go into a relationship loving some idealistic, future version of the person, someone you think you can fashion out of the mess you see. If you can't love the mess in front of you, don't marry it in the first place.

If the person you are with is not the person you know they could be, your natural reaction might be to pressure them to change—for their good and yours—into the image you have in your head. Your motives might be noble, but your methods are going to drive one or both of you crazy. You can't nag someone into changing. Nobody wants to marry their parent, their boss, their babysitter. You are partners in this thing called marriage, and partners deserve respect and the autonomy to change as they see fit.

God will work on your significant other, but it's not up to you to dictate when or how that happens, nor to demand they change in a particular way. Your focus needs to be on what you can change in yourself. Jesus said, "How can you think of saying, 'Friend, let me help you get rid of that speck in your eye,' when you can't see past the log in your own eye?'" (Luke 6:42 NLT). You'll find a lot more grace in your relationship (and more humility and patience in your own heart) if you focus on areas in which *you* can grow and leave your significant other in God's hands.

Instead of making them change for you, focus on what you can change for them. Become the person they need. The spouse they can depend on. The boyfriend or girlfriend with whom they feel safe and loved.

Put simply, stop looking for the other person to become the person you're looking for, and become the person the person you're looking for is looking for. Okay, that isn't simple at all. But if you read it slowly, it makes sense. I promise.

5. HOW DO YOU SPEAK TO THE ONE YOU LOVE?

It's fascinating to me how different people get mad in different ways. Some shut down, some lash out, some walk away, some simmer until they explode, and so on.

I'm a talker, so if I have a problem with someone, I'd rather talk it out. And by "talk," I mean converse intensely and emotionally at a high volume. Not yelling—just really, really engaged.

DawnCheré prefers to stay silent while she gets her emotions under control and figures out what she's going to say. Yet another reason why she's the smart one in our relationship. That doesn't mean she's not mad—trust me, I know when she's mad—it just means she processes anger differently than I do.

During the early years of our relationship, I remember having "discussions" a few different times while we were driving. I'd say something that upset her, and then instead of apologizing or trying to meet her in the middle, I'd attempt to prove why I was right. Eventually, she'd just clam up. She'd stop looking at me, stop talking to me, and simply stare out of the windshield with a glare icy enough to make Miami freeze over.

It would get to me pretty quickly. "DawnCheré," I'd say, "you've got to talk to me. Come on, let's work this out."

She wouldn't say anything, but the look on her face was always clear enough. *I can't even look at you right now. You think I'm going to talk to you?*

We're better at arguing now. In a good way. Working through differences is a learned skill, one that every couple will need to use more often than they might expect. You have to understand how to respond to the other person in a healthy way, even when tensions are high. *Especially* when tensions are high, actually, because that's when we tend to be the most careless.

The words you say and the way you say them create the environment for your life together. Scripture states, "Gracious words are a honeycomb, sweet to the soul and healing to the bones," and, "The tongue has the power of life and death, and those who love it will eat its fruit" (Proverbs 16:24, 18:21).

How do you speak to each other? Words and tone matter so much, and they are an important indicator of your relational health.

- Does your word choice demonstrate respect for each other?
- Do you both have a chance to talk?

How do you speak to each other? Words and tone matter so much, and they are an important indicator of your relational health.

- Do you know how to express your feelings?
- Can you empathize with the other person's point of view even when you disagree?
- Are you emotionally intelligent, able to manage your emotions in positive ways?
- Are you willing to ask for forgiveness and to grant forgiveness?
- Do you listen to understand or listen looking for ammunition for your reply?
- Do you leave the past in the past or bring it up to get your way?
- Do you focus on what unites you or what separates you?
- Do you learn from each other?
- Do you laugh together?

Too often, arguments become a nuclear war of sarcasm, name-calling, and accusations. It usually starts because you feel hurt by them. So you try to hurt them back. Then they hurt you even more and the whole thing devolves into a vicious cycle that wounds both of you and accomplishes nothing. Other times, communication breaks down completely. You become enemies in a cold war, unwilling to humble yourself or restore broken lines of communication. Neither of these two extremes—nuclear war or cold war—is helpful.

DawnCheré and I aren't perfect at this, but we learned a long time ago that neither intense debates nor glaring out of windshields were going to get us what we actually wanted: a healthy relationship. We have to work together, not against each other. We have to attack the problem, not one another.

Words create the future, and how you speak to each other sets the course for your relationship.

6. DO YOU WANT A GOOD RELATIONSHIP OR A GREAT ONE?

Author and researcher Jim Collins has done extensive research on why certain companies become truly great. In his classic business book *Good to Great,* he writes:

> Good is the enemy of great.
> And that is one of the key reasons why we have so little that becomes great.
> We don't have great schools, principally because we have good schools. We don't have great government, principally because we have good government. Few people attain great lives, in large part because it is just so easy to settle for a good life.[19]

Applied to a dating relationship or marriage, you might settle for good when God wants to give you great.

Whether you have a good relationship or a great one is mostly a matter of vision and the willingness to persevere toward that vision. What do you want to achieve? What will you settle for? These are not questions meant to condemn anyone because no relationship is perfect. But relationships are not static, either. They change. They grow. And if you have a vision for a great marriage, you'll refuse to settle for mediocrity and instead pursue the dream you see.

Years ago, DawnCheré and I asked ourselves, "What culture do we want in our home?" We started throwing out some words. We started naming things we wanted to see become a reality in our marriage.

For example, we decided we wanted a house full of adventure, a home that is spontaneous. From then on, we were intentional about relishing life in the moment, about doing things that were important but maybe outside our comfort zone, about facing new stages of life with excitement. We've always had a motto: *If you're afraid of it, run toward it.* So when either of us says, "I'm nervous about that; I'm scared to do it," the other will say, "You can do, go for it, you've got this."

We decided we wanted a home full of encouragement, one where people would leave feeling lighter and happier and more excited about life than when they walked in. We wanted a welcoming home where people would know they are accepted and loved. Those are just a few of the words we chose. The point isn't the words as much as it is the choice. The vision. The decision to strive for a certain culture and environment.

Again, no home or marriage or person is perfect, so you have to keep things in perspective. You might be dating someone who is 80 percent awesome and 20 percent not so awesome. Don't overreact. Sometimes people want to bail on a relationship because of the 20 percent they don't like, and they find out too late how valuable the 80 percent they did like actually was. Then they move on to someone else, and they find that person also has 20 percent (or 30 percent or 40 percent) that isn't so great.

That said, don't give up on improving the 20 percent, if you can. You can't force anyone to change (as we saw above), but you can work together toward a vision for a better relationship—whatever that looks like to you.

7. WHY IS IT YOUR GOAL TO BE RIGHT?

"I told you so" has to be one of the most toxic phrases in any relationship. Maybe you've learned this the hard way. Your significant other wanted to do things his way, and it didn't work out, and you gloated a bit. For some reason, that didn't go over well.

Or your girlfriend was sure she was right about something, but you Googled it, and it turns out she was wrong. So you pointed that out. Gleefully. You won the argument but lost the war because she stomped out and left you alone with your phone and your smugness.

If the argument is over something dumb, it probably doesn't matter that much. One or both of you were obnoxious, but you're still lovable and in love, and the two of you will move on. But when the issues are bigger, an "I'm right, you're wrong" attitude can be absolutely destructive. For example, if the other person failed in a business venture, the last thing they probably need is a loved one to rake them over the coals for it. They know they failed. They need love, forgiveness, and faith for the future, not more shame. Instead of, "I told you so," they need to hear, "You did your best and I'm proud of you. Things will work out better next time."

Being right doesn't help anything in a relationship. It's a terrible goal. It makes every issue personal. It makes every argument a war. It amplifies shame and shatters trust. It polarizes two people instead of uniting them.

Being right is not a fruit of the Spirit. Patience is, and joy is, and self-control is. Those are the things that should show up in your words and your expressions when one of you is wrong, not some self-serving reminder that they should have listened

If the argument is over something dumb, it probably doesn't matter that much. One or both of you were obnoxious, but you're still lovable and in love, and the two of you will move on. *move on*

to you. Over the long term, an insistence on being right and proving the other person wrong eats away at trust and respect, which are foundational to all relationships. If you walk that path long enough, you'll end up right and alone.

Why do we take failure so seriously, anyway? Failure is a necessary step toward growth. Being wrong from time to time is the inevitable result of taking risks and moving forward. Give people space to learn and grow. Applaud their courage rather than judging their mistakes. Yes, share your wisdom and ideas; and yes, learn from mistakes. But do those things from a heart of unity, not a place of pride.

A desire to be right shuts you off from learning from someone else. Instead of listening, you just plan your rebuttal. Your brain can think a lot faster than it can hear, so it's easy to jump ahead to what you want to say rather than engaging fully with the other person's words and emotions.

Slow down.

Listen.

Learn.

That's far more important than proving your point. What can you do instead of fighting to be right?

Recognize your own bias. Bias means your predisposition toward something. Nobody is neutral. Bias is normal—it becomes bad when you ignore it. Be aware of the values, fears, experiences, assumptions, and emotions that are informing your own opinion.

Admit where you are wrong. Being able to say, "I'm sorry; I was wrong," brings true intimacy. It also gives you credibility to be a little more insistent when you really are right.

Recognize common ground. Unite around what you agree on, which usually is nearly everything, then resolve differences starting from there.

Negotiate a compromise. This validates and honors the other person, and it recognizes the value of their point of view. This isn't weakness; it's wisdom.

Find a third option. Use pushback from the other person to discover the weaknesses or blind spots in your own perspective, then work together to find a solution that takes both of your perspectives into account.

Know when to give in. Not every hill is a hill to die on. Learn when to let the other person make the decision. Then avoid second-guessing or micromanaging them.

Working together in this way does more than just avoid conflict or keep the peace. It builds a wise, strong home and family. It creates trust, respect, and intimacy. It protects you against wrong decisions or one-sided leadership in the family. It fosters a safe culture, making the home a place of acceptance and security. Being right is overrated; humility, patience, and mercy are invaluable.

8. WHERE DO YOU HAVE THE MOST FUN?

"Fun" tends to be underestimated in relationships, especially after marriage. Maybe it doesn't sound holy enough, mature enough, or serious enough. I don't know. Whatever the reason, though, don't take relationships so seriously that you forget to have fun. Or, to say it another way, take seriously the importance of having fun in your relationship.

Love should be relatively easy. Not all the time, but for the most part. You should want to be with the other person. You should enjoy talking to them. You should have a lot of shared values and at least a few shared interests.

If the fun is gone from your relationship, you need to ask why. Where did it go? Why did it stop? And what can you do to get it back?

Having fun together produces joy, and joy brings strength. The prophet Nehemiah said, "The joy of the Lord is your strength" (Nehemiah 8:10). The author was talking about God's joy and the supernatural strength that comes from him, but the principle is true on a human level, too.

Couples that play together stay together. Couples that laugh together can go through pain together. Couples that enjoy each other's company during times of peace won't storm out of the room (or out of the relationship) during a fight.

Remember, you aren't just supposed to *love* the person you're with; you're supposed to *like* them, too. Don't be so spiritual and serious and sacrificial that you forget to have fun together. Fun creates joy; joy builds strength; strength gives you protection.

So ask yourself some fun questions. Where do we have the most fun? What do we like to do together? When do we most enjoy being together? Identify those things. Try some new ones. Get creative.

Keep in mind that you can have fun doing things together even if they aren't exactly a favorite activity for one of you. Most couples don't have identical hobbies or tastes. Yet, there is something beautiful about entering into whatever it is that brings joy and delight to the other person.

DawnCheré and I are totally different. I like scary, adventurous action movies. She likes only romantic comedies. I love the ocean and the beach. She doesn't like salt water. I could go on. But we've learned to compromise and do a lot of things together, and because of that, we have an ever-growing list of fun, shared memories.

A few years ago, I was speaking at an event in London. I found out the Broadway musical *Singing in the Rain* was showing. I'll be honest, I don't really like musicals. I don't understand why everyone sings instead of just talking. It seems so inefficient. If you were to take out the songs, there would be about eight minutes of real action. That's a lot like an NFL game, I guess. Anyway, musicals are DawnCheré's love language. So I told her, "I'm taking you to see *Singing in the Rain.*" It was a sacrifice of love, for sure. But I've never seen DawnCheré so excited. She was freaking out, and it was awesome.

What happened there? I simply put myself into her space and said, "I'm going to go into your world and do something you like. We're in this together, and we're going to have fun."

DawnCheré does the same thing for me. She doesn't do salt water, as I mentioned, but I love to scuba dive. She won't go under water with me, but after I finish, she'll say, "Rich, how was it? Tell me about all the scuba diving stuff. Is it like *Little Mermaid*?" (Again with the musicals, right?) I know she doesn't care that much, but she cares about me, and that means a lot to me.

Parents do this, too, with their children. If you don't have children, but you are the cool uncle or the fun aunt to nieces or nephews, you might have done this as well. You go into the kids' world. You play with their toys, you listen to their stories, you find joy in what makes them happy. You don't expect them to enter your boring adult world. You make an effort to have fun their way.

If you're dating or married, enjoy it! Have fun. Play. Goof off. Sing karaoke or go dancing or skydive or scale a mountain or take up couples' yoga or go on a picnic or see Broadway musicals or do whatever you want. Just don't let the fun leak out of the relationship. Don't let it get squashed by busyness, bitterness, or stress.

Dating is fun. Marriage is fun. Sex is fun. Kids are fun.

Love is fun.

Don't let anyone tell you otherwise.

LOVE is FUN!

9. ARE YOU FOCUSED ON WHAT YOU CAN GET OR WHAT YOU CAN GIVE?

In his 1961 inaugural address, John F. Kennedy famously said, "Ask not what your country can do for you—ask what you can do for your country." I would say the same principle applies to your relationship. Ask not what your significant other can do for you, but what you can do for your significant other.

Generosity makes your world bigger, and it makes you bigger. The writer of Proverbs stated, "The world of the generous gets larger and larger; the world of the stingy gets smaller and smaller" (Proverbs 11:24 MSG). Jesus taught, "It is more blessed to give than to receive" (Acts 20:35). If you want a big life, a life full of wide-open spaces, joy, peace, adventure, and purpose—be generous.

Sometimes the pain of relationships or the failures of a loved one can tempt you to retreat into yourself. To withhold yourself until the other person proves themselves. To say, "They don't treat me well, they don't show me love, they don't give to me, so I'm going to treat them the same way."

Why don't you go first? Why don't you show them love first? What if you took a month just to see what would happen if you spoke love, honor, and faith into that person's life every day? I've mentioned before that you should not allow toxic or abusive behavior to continue, so please know that I'm not talking about that. Love does not mean martyrdom, nor does it mean enabling an abuser. But it does mean being willing to give first. That's what love does—it gives. It helps. It builds. It serves.

Happiness is a funny thing. It's elusive. If you try to get it for yourself, you usually find yourself clutching at air. That is why if you go into love thinking it has to make you happy all the time, you'll miss out on the joys of relationship.

Instead, love first, and you'll find happiness and fulfillment as you go along. They aren't the goal, but they are a beautiful byproduct, because it's always more blessed to give than to receive.

10. HAVE YOU DECIDED ON YOUR FIRST PRIORITY?

On one of our fist dates, DawnCheré and I drew a triangle on a piece of paper. At the top of the triangle we wrote the name "Jesus." On the other two points, we wrote "Rich" and "DawnCheré." We said that if we made our priority Jesus, we would always meet in the middle, at the top of the triangle.

It sounds so innocent, maybe even cheesy. But a few years into our marriage, we have the same priority. The same decision. God is first, and because God is first, we grow closer and closer together. That's the only kind of love triangle we are interested in.

Earlier I referenced a Bible passage that lists the ways in which "two are better than one". Here is the full list:

> Two are better than one,
> because they have a good return for their labor:
> If either of them falls down,
> one can help the other up.
> But pity anyone who falls
> and has no one to help them up.
> Also, if two lie down together, they will keep warm.

> But how can one keep warm alone?
> Though one may be overpowered,
> two can defend themselves.
> A cord of three strands is not quickly broken.
> (Ecclesiastes 4:9-12)

This passage is a beautiful picture of the strength that comes through the uniting of two lives. The last phrase, though, makes a subtle switch. It says, "A cord of three strands is not quickly broken" (Ecclesiastes 4:12). The whole passage is about two, two, two, and now suddenly it's about three.

To me, this speaks about two lives joined together in God. He is the third strand braided into the cord. And when two lives are intertwined with his, the relationship can withstand anything.

This is vital to understand because you will go through some hard things together. There will be fights. There will be valleys. There will be moments of doubt. There will be times when the feelings hide for a while because that's what feelings do.

If you make Jesus your priority, though, if you find your completeness and direction in him, if you pursue his will and his value system, then you'll be like that cord of three strands. Tested, but not broken. Tried, but not unraveled. Taut, but not snapped in two. Jesus will sustain your relationship.

If you're single, what's your first priority? You might say, "To fall in love! To find someone I can settle down with." That's not a great top priority. That's a good secondary priority, maybe, but your top pursuit, your greatest desire, should be to know God and to follow him. He's the only one who makes life make sense. He's the only one who can give you value. He's the only one who can see the future and guide you into it.

This is why it's so valuable to marry someone who shares your spiritual values. If both of you are seeking God, your relationship will be in good hands. That's all you can ask for because you don't know the future and you can't control it anyway.

Nobody is ever ready for marriage. Nobody knows what they're getting into. Nobody fully knows the other person, and even if they did, that person will change with time. But if you know God, and if he is your primary pursuit, you don't have to stress about things you can't control anyway. God will guide you both. His grace will infuse your marriage with life and wisdom. You'll change when you need to change, and your partner will too. You'll both follow God's leading, you'll grow to be more like him, and in the process, you'll grow closer and closer together.

***

Whether you are single, engaged, or married, you need to continually evaluate your approach to relationships. Not with a terrified, I-might-mess-this-up mentality, but with the confidence that comes from knowing God wants to lead you into a healthy, stable future. You can always learn more, and you can always grow. That's one of the greatest things about being a human.

To be sure, it takes work to have healthy relationships—that's the whole point behind these ten questions. For that matter, it's one of the main points of this entire book. It takes courage, and love, and risk, and patience, and probably some trial and error.

But it is well worth it all.

Even if you've gone through some complicated relationships, don't give up on finding love. Even if you've failed loved ones in the past, don't give up on being a good friend or lover. Even if you've experienced abuse, trauma, or abandonment, don't give up on people.

Turn to God. Let him bring healing, hope, and love. Let him give you security and strength in who you are. And then, as he leads you forward, be willing to embrace new and better ways of relating to people.

As I've said throughout this book, those people may or may

You don't have to be single and stuck. Single and desperate. Single and bitter. Single and embarrassed. Single and defensive. Single and frustrated.

You are single and secure.

YOU ARE!

not include a spouse or children. Singleness, marriage, parenting, or any other age, stage, or label doesn't define you. Only God gets to do that, and he is happy with where you are and with who you are. Whether you believe that and live in alignment with it, is up to you. You must decide to be secure and to make the most of every day.

You don't have to be single and stuck. Single and desperate. Single and bitter. Single and embarrassed. Single and defensive. Single and frustrated.

You are single and secure.

THE PATH AHEAD

Your best days are not the ones that lie far in the future, after you find a spouse or build your career or start a business. Your best days are the ones you live to the fullest.

That starts now.

I don't mean to say the journey will be easy. It will have its share of painful moments and frustrating experiences. Life is unpredictable, after all, and none of us can even see the path ahead, much less control it.

There's a beautiful Scripture verse that always encourages me: "The path of the righteous is like the morning sun, shining ever brighter till the full light of day" (Proverbs 4:18). In other words, things will get better and better. Your best days are now—but they are also coming, because with God, your world will grow bigger and become fuller as time goes on.

Again, that's not the same thing as saying it will get easier and easier. Buying a home is not easy. Chasing toddlers is not easy. Building a business is not easy. Living with integrity is not easy. Picking out a birthday present, Christmas present, Valentines' Day present, Mother's Day present, anniversary present, and "just because" presents every single year for the rest of your life is not only not easy, it is freaking impossible. God help me. But I digress.

Easy is not the goal, though. The goal is to make the most of the life that's been given to you. To love God and love the people around you. To laugh a lot more and stress out a little less. To choose gratitude over bitterness, joy over resentment, patience over frustration, love over selfishness. The goal is to live in security and confidence in God and in yourself.

You already have what you need to be secure: God's grace, the power to choose, and a sense of humor. Oh, and coffee. What else could you want?

You've got this.

WORKS CITED

[1] Lesley Gore, "It's My Party," Mercury Records, 1963.

[2] Brené Brown, *The Gifts of Imperfection* (Center City, MN: Hazelden Publishing, 2010), 40.

[3] Brown, The Gifts of Imperfection.

[4] Oprah Winfrey, "The Queen of Daytime TV," interview with Oprah Winfrey, Academy of Achievement, February 25, 1991, https://achievement.org/achiever/oprah-winfrey/#interview.

[5] John C. Maxwell, *The 21 Irrefutable Laws of Leadership: Follow Them and People Will Follow You* (Nashville, TN: HarperCollins Leadership, 1998, 2007), 103.

[6] C. S. Lewis, *The Screwtape Letters* (New York: HarperCollins, 1942, 1959, 1982), XX.

[7] Coleman Cox, *Listen to This* (San Francisco: Coleman Cox Publishing Co., 1922), VII.

[8] Rick Warren, *The Purpose-Driven Life: What on Earth Am I Here For? Expanded Edition* (Grand Rapids, MI: Zondervan, 2002, 2011, 2012), 262.

[9] Craig Groeschel (@craiggroeschel). Twitter, September 26, 2018, https://twitter.com/craiggroeschel/status/1045112287676239872

[10] Often attributed to Neil Barringham. For example: https://www.osmquote.com/quote/neil-barringham-quote-54c4b8

[11] Charles Swindoll, quoted in *Wisdom for the Soul: Five Millennia of Prescriptions for Spiritual Healing*, Larry Chang, ed. (Washington, DC: Gnosophia Publishers, 2006), 72.

[12] Marie Kondo, "What Is the KonMari Method?", KonMarie, undated, https://shop.konmari.com/pages/about.

[13] C.S. Lewis, *Mere Christianity* (New York: Touchstone, 1996), 115.

[14] C.S. Lewis, *Four Loves* (New York: Harcourt, Brace, Jovanovich, 1960), 169.

[15] James R. Sherman, *Rejection* (Golden Valley, MN: Pathway Books, 1982), 45.

[16] Andy Stanley, *The New Rules for Love, Sex, and Dating.* (Grand Rapids, MI: Zondervan, 2014), XX.

[17] Virginia Pelley, "What Is the Divorce Rate in America?" *Fatherly*, February 25, 2021, https://www.fatherly.com/love-money/what-is-divorce-rate-america/.

[18] Alain da Botton, "Why You Will Marry the Wrong Person" *New York Times*, May 28, 2016, http://nyti.ms/1RAnp1X.

[19] Jim Collins, Good to Great: Why Some Companies Make the Leap...and Others Don't (New York: HarperBusiness, 2001), 1.

ABOUT THE AUTHOR

Rich Wilkerson Jr. and his wife DawnCheré lead VOUS Church, a community of faith in the heart of Miami committed to loving God and serving people. Rich is the author of three books: *Sandcastle Kings, Friend of Sinners,* and *Single & Secure*. After an eight-year journey of infertility, Rich and DawnCheré have welcomed three children into their family: Wyatt, Wilde, and Waylon.

@richwilkersonjr

Text me: 305-501-1890

intothenight.com

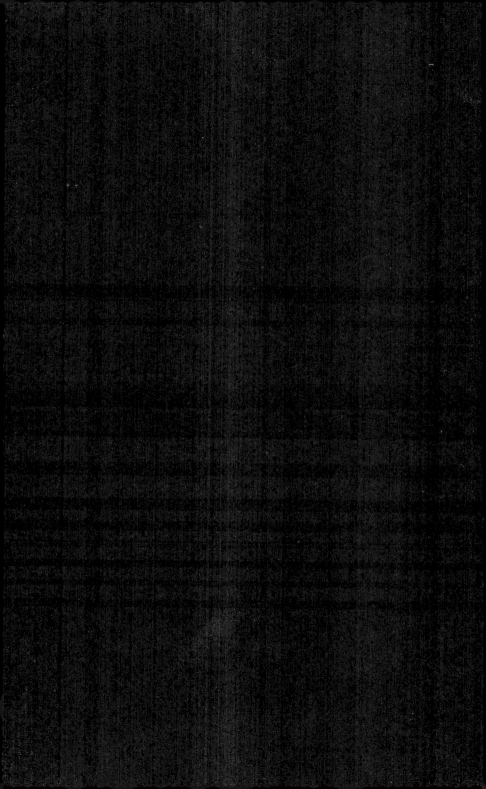